:30 MINUTE EARRINGS

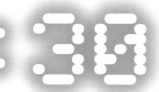 MINUTE EARRINGS

► **60 Quick & Creative Projects for Jewelers**

Marthe Le Van

 LARK CRAFTS

An Imprint of Sterling Publishing Co., Inc.
New York

WWW.LARKCRAFTS.COM

Assistant Editor
Gavin R. Young

Art Director
Kristi Pfeffer

Art Production Assistant
Bradley Norris

Photographer
Stewart O'Shields

Cover Designers
Celia Naranjo and Chris Bryant

Library of Congress Cataloging-in-Publication Data

Le Van, Marthe.
    30-minute earrings : 60 quick & creative projects for jewelers / Marthe Le Van.
        p. cm.
    Includes bibliographical references and index.
    ISBN 978-1-60059-487-8 (pb-pbk. : alk. paper)
    1. Jewelry making. I. Title. II. Title: Thirty-minute earrings.
    TT212.L488 2010
    739.27--dc22

                         2009037360

10 9 8 7 6 5 4 3 2

Published by Lark Crafts, An Imprint of
Sterling Publishing Co., Inc.
387 Park Avenue South, New York, NY 10016

Distributed in Canada by Sterling Publishing,
c/o Canadian Manda Group, 165 Dufferin Street
Toronto, Ontario, Canada M6K 3H6

Distributed in the United Kingdom by GMC Distribution Services,
Castle Place, 166 High Street, Lewes, East Sussex, England BN7 1XU

Distributed in Australia by Capricorn Link (Australia) Pty Ltd.,
P.O. Box 704, Windsor, NSW 2756 Australia

If you have questions or comments about this book, please contact:
Lark Crafts
67 Broadway
Asheville, NC 28801
828-253-0467

Manufactured in China

ISBN 13: 978-1-60059-487-8

For information about custom editions, special sales, premium and corporate purchases, please contact Sterling Special Sales Department at 800-805-5489 or specialsales@sterlingpub.com.

For information about desk and examination copies available to college and university professors, requests must be submitted to academic@larkbooks.com. Our complete policy can be found at www.larkcrafts.com.

CONTENTS

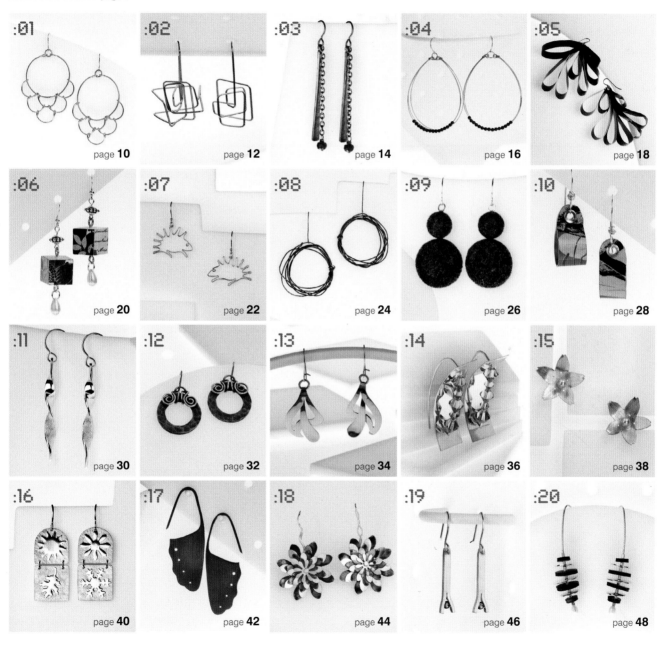

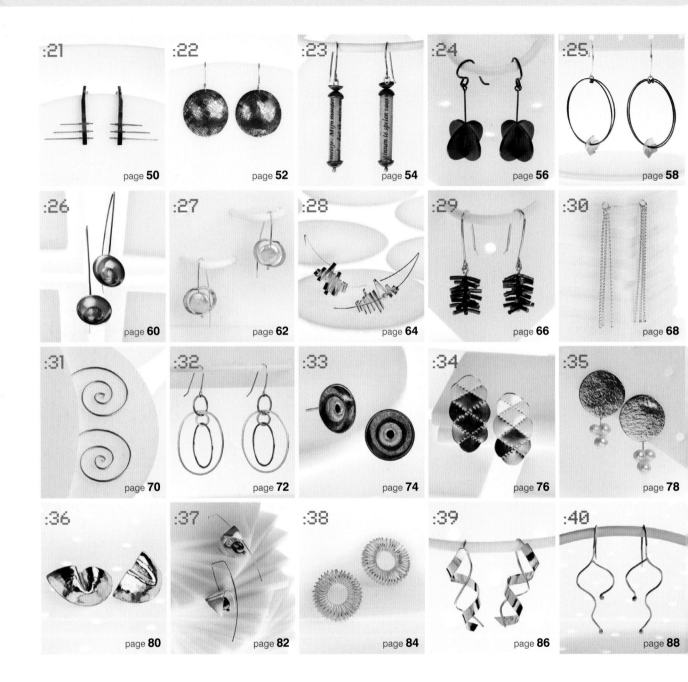

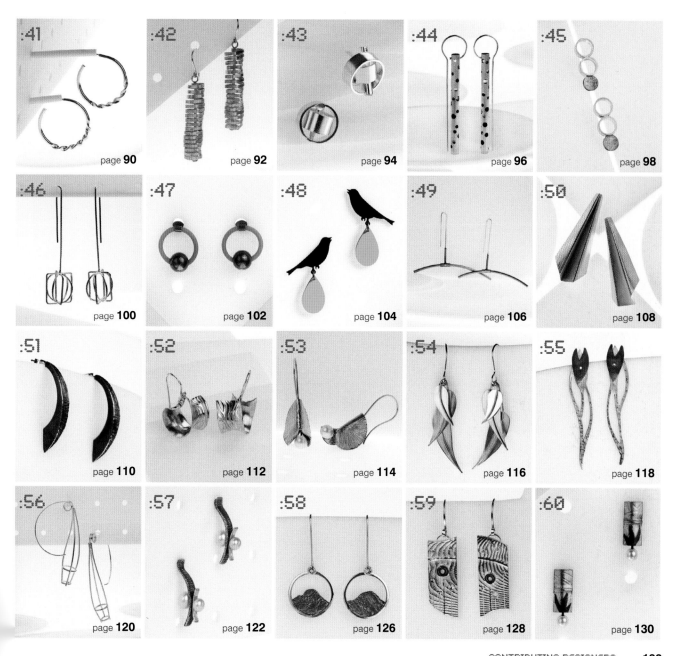

Introduction

There never seems to be enough time in the day, especially for the precious element of play. But, as this book will attest, a lot can happen in 30 minutes. We invited top designers to break down the barriers that time itself builds up: barriers like self consciousness, over-analytical thinking, voices whispering "try it a different way," and a hundred other obstacles that can get in the way of pure creativity. We presented a challenge. Sit down at your jeweler's bench and start the clock. Create a pair of earrings in 30 minutes flat, and just do it. Let go.

The results are astounding. The variety of materials, array of techniques, and range of styles in *30-Minute Earrings* are nothing short of brilliant. Some projects are nature-inspired; some have geometric structure; others are derived from animals or include found objects in their construction. Consider designer Laura Itkoken who presented us with videotape earrings (page 18). She chose a retro material to be the champion of her design, and let it speak for itself. The techniques are simple: pierce holes in videotape, loop it into a desired shape, and attach earring hooks. But the form looks complex, vibrant, and incredibly modern.

The flip side to this approach is a pair of elegant, classic earrings by Deborah Fehrenbach (page 62). She selected traditional materials such as sterling silver and coin pearls, but employed soldering and forging, skills that are a little more involved. Whatever the method practiced by our 45 designers, the 60 projects they share in these pages will wow you, inspire you, and motivate you to drop everything else for 30 minutes and engage in this exhilarating exercise.

Know what else is exhilarating? Earrings that don't take long to make don't cost much either. In these tricky economic times, it's a rush to make your own jewelry that looks as if it was purchased in a high-end boutique for a top-dollar price. If you're a working jeweler, you probably already have the tools needed for most of the projects. If you're a new designer, you'll be surprised at how many earrings you can create with just a few basic tools: a jeweler's saw, hammer, pliers, wire snips, and sandpaper will carry you a long way. Because earrings are relatively small, you won't be investing much on materials, and you may even have many of them lying around in your studio or workroom. Got scrap metal? Fabulous! How about a stash of findings, old fabric swatches, or leftover wire? Even better!

Depending on your skill level, you may feel more comfortable brushing up on some basic metalworking techniques, materials, and tools before you start a project. If so, *The Ultimate Jeweler's Guide* by Joanna Gollberg,

whose earrings are featured on page 12, is a great refer-
ence. She explains everything from cold connections and
hot joining, to forming and finishing techniques. While her
book is more how-to, *30-Minute Earrings* is all about get
ready, get set, go! In fact, that's exactly how we've struc-
tured each set of instructions. Under **Get Ready** headings,
you'll see a short list of skills required to complete the
project. Under **Get Set**, the designer presents you with
the necessary tools and materials. When you reach the
heading that precedes step-by-step instructions, you'll be
raring to **Go**!

So, what are you waiting for? Step outside yourself, trust
your instincts, and turn the page. The clock is ticking.

Bench Tool Kit

Bench pin

Steel bench block

Jeweler's saw frame

Saw blades

Beeswax

Needle files

Bastard file

Sandpaper,
    220 and 400 grit

Emery paper

Chasing hammer

Rawhide or wooden
    mallet

Forging hammer

Mandrels

Dapping block and
    punches

Flexible shaft

Wood block

Drill bits

Burrs

Separating disk

Scribe

Stainless steel ruler

Dividers

Calipers

Pliers

Wire cutters

Center punch

Burnisher

Safety glasses

Safety gloves

Hearing protection

Dust mask

Soldering Kit

Soldering torch

Striker

Heat resistant soldering
    surface (charcoal
    blocks, firebricks,
    or ceramic plates)

Flux

Flux brush or other
    applicator

Solder (hard, medium,
    and easy)

Snips

Small embroidery
    scissors

Solder pick

Tweezers

Cross-locking tweezers
    with wooden handle

Third hand

Copper tongs

Water for quenching

Pickle

Pickle warming pot

Safety glasses

Fire extinguisher

▶▶ ▶ Get Set

Brass or brass-coated wire, 16 gauge, approximately 40 inches (91.4 cm)

2 brass- or gold-plated ear wires

Flush cutters

Small file

Round-nose pliers

Dowel, glass, or bottle (optional)

Flat-nose or chain-nose pliers, 2 pairs

FINISHED SIZE
Each, 7 x 4.4 cm, not including findings

DESIGNER'S NOTE
Create your own ear wires from 20-gauge brass wire if desired.

▶ ▶ ▶ Go

1. Using flush cutters, cut twelve 2-inch (5.1 cm) pieces and two 6-inch (15.2 cm) pieces from the 16-gauge brass wire. File the ends of each cut wire piece flat and smooth.

2. With round-nose pliers, form a small loop on each end of one 2-inch (5.1 cm) wire piece. Don't center the loops on the wire; just fold over the ends. Make sure the loops on each end line up with each other. Repeat with the other 2-inch (5.1 cm) pieces of brass wire.

3. Grasp one 2-inch (5.1 cm) wire, and start bending it into an arch with your fingers. Run your fingers along the wire and ease it into shape, or bend it around a dowel or the top of a bottle. The final shape should be arched, but not quite a half-circle.

4. Using the flat-nose pliers, grab the wire loop at one end of the arched wire and bend it towards the middle of the arch. (When you assemble these arched wires to create the earring, they hang downwards; the two loops on each one should be straight up and down so that you can thread them onto the larger loop.)

5. With the round-nose pliers, bend both ends of each 6-inch (15.2 cm) piece of wire into medium-sized loops. Center these end loops on the wires. Bend each wire into a full circle, using a bottle, glass, or dowel if needed. (The end loops on each circle should meet but just barely touch. The loops will rest perpendicular to the plane of each circle.)

6. Make two jump rings from the 16-gauge wire, each approximately ¼ inch (0.6 cm) in diameter. File the edges of the rings flush. Use one jump ring to connect the two loops on each large wire hoop.

7. Determine which side of each large hoop will face front. Open the loops on all the 2-inch (5.1 cm) arched wire pieces.

8. To assemble the earrings, connect three of the arched wire pieces side by side onto the large hoop, positioning them so that the loops all face toward the back of the hoop.

9. Connect the loops of another arched wire to the first and second pieces added in step 8. Add another arched wire to the second and third pieces added in step 8.

10. To complete the scaled look, connect a final arched wire piece to the ones added in step 9. Repeat steps 8 through 10 to assemble the other earring. Connect an ear wire to the jump ring at the top of each large hoop.

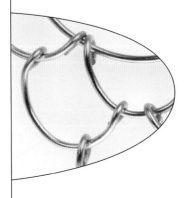

→ ► Get Set

Sterling silver, gold,
  or stainless steel wire,
  18 or 20 gauge, 24 to 36
  inches (61 to 91.4 cm)

Bench tool kit, page 9

Vise

FINISHED SIZE
Variable

Examples shown
Left, 3.5 x 2.5 x 2.5 cm
Right, 4 x 2.3 x 2.5 cm
Below, 3.7 x 3.7 x 2.5 cm

DESIGNER'S NOTE
These earrings are so quick
to make, you can do a test
run with scrap wire first
and still finish a pair in 30
minutes.

→ ► ► Go

1. Cut a length of wire that is 12 to 18 inches (30.5 to 45.7 cm) long.

2. Insert the end of the wire into a vise. Grasp the other end of the wire with pliers. Pull gently but firmly to slightly stretch the wire and straighten it.

3. Measure approximately 1½ to 2 inches (3.8 to 5.1 cm) from one end of the wire. Hold the wire with needle-nose pliers at that point, and bend the long tail over with your finger to create a right angle.

4. Continue bending the wire at different angles and at different lengths to achieve an architectural structure.

5. Repeat steps 1 through 4 to create a second earring.

6. Form the ear wires from the 1½ to 2-inch (3.8 to 5.1 cm) sections measured in step 3. Either bend these sections of wire at right angles to go through the ear or round them over a mandrel, pen, or other tubular object. Make sure the ear wires are long enough to prevent the earrings from falling out of the ear.

7. Sand the ends of the ear wires smooth.

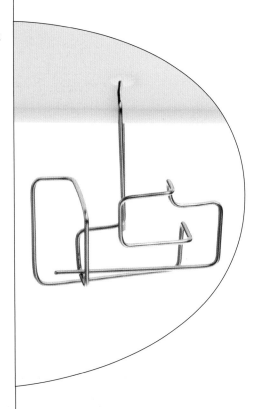

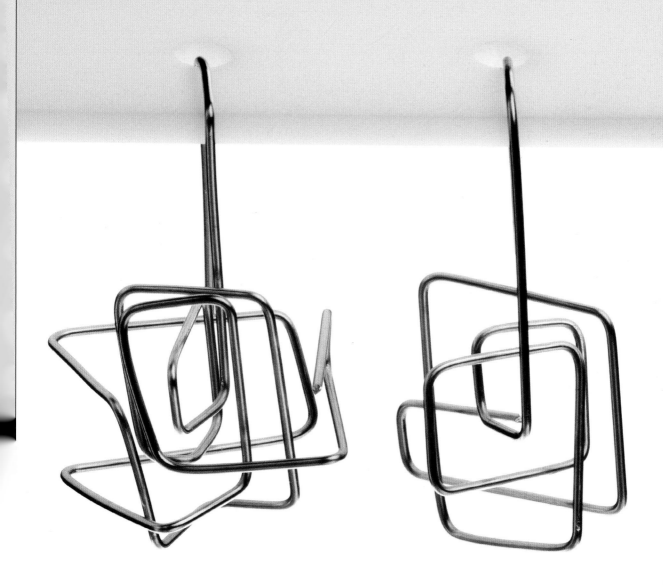

DESIGNERS: **TAYA AND SILVIJA KOSCHNICK**

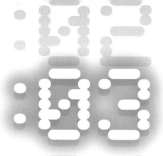

▶ ▶ Get Set

Sterling silver cable chain,
2 x 3 mm, 8.9 cm long

2 sterling silver ball
headpins, 26 gauge

2 grey niobium ear wires

2 vintage brass dangles,
each 4.5 x 1.4 cm

2 ruby rondelles, 3 x 4 mm

Bench tool kit, page 9

Liver of sulfur (optional)

Fine steel wool

FINISHED SIZE
Each, 5 x 0.5 x 0.4 cm

TIME SAVER
If you purchase pre-oxidized
cable chain and headpins,
you can go straight to step 2.

▶ ▶ ▶ Go

1. Blacken the sterling silver cable chain
and headpins in a liver of sulfur solution.

2. Cut the cable chain into two 4.4-cm
pieces.

3. Open the niobium ear wires with pliers
and attach the brass dangle and a length of
chain. Close the ear wires.

4. String a ruby rondelle onto each ball
headpin. Thread one headpin through the
bottom link of each chain, and wrap the end
of the headpin around itself, just above the
rondelle. Snip off any excess wire.

5. Gently rub the chains and headpins with
fine steel wool until the desired patina is
achieved.

WIREWORK • BEAD STRINGING

▶▶ **Get Set**

Round brass wire,
   24 gauge, 5 feet (1.5 m)

30 lapis lazuli round beads,
   4 mm

2 gold-plated jump rings,
   7 mm

2 gold-plated ear wires

Bench tool kit, page 9

FINISHED SIZE
Each hoop, 7 x 5.5 x 0.4 cm

▶▶▶ **Go**

1. Using side-cutting pliers, cut six pieces of brass wire, each 9 inches (22.9 cm) long.

2. Hold three of the wire pieces side by side so that you can bend them simultaneously. Use round-nose pliers to create a loop in the gathered wires, about 1 inch (2.5 cm) from one end. Wrap the tail around the loop, and clip off the excess wire. Use flat-nose pliers to bend the edges into a neatly formed, wrapped loop.

3. Slide 15 lapis beads onto the middle wire. Using round-nose pliers, make another wrapped loop at the other end of the three wires.

4. Use chain-nose pliers to open a jump ring. Slide both wrapped loops onto the jump ring to form a teardrop shape. Slip an ear wire onto the jump ring, and close the jump ring.

5. Repeat steps 1 through 4 to make the second earring.

DESIGNER: **LAURA ITKONEN**

►► Get Set

VHS videotape

2 silver jump rings, 20 gauge, 10 mm in diameter

2 silver jump rings, 20 gauge, 6.5 mm in diameter

2 silver earring hooks

Screwdriver

Pointed pliers

Needle or straight pin

Flat pliers

Scissors

FINISHED SIZE
Each, 7.5 x 6.5 x 1.3 cm

►►► Go

1. Open the VHS videotape with a screwdriver and pull out the tape.

2. Open the 10-mm silver jump rings with pliers.

3. Using a needle or straight pin, make a hole about 4 mm from one end of the videotape and centered across its width.

4. Slip an opened 10-mm silver jump ring through the hole, handling the tape with care.

5. Determine how large to make the first tape loop on the earring. Then, pierce another hole in the tape and slip the tape onto the silver ring. (On this project, this second hole is about 6 cm from the first.) Repeat this process to form a series of tape loops on the jump ring, sizing them in any way you like. Note: If you'd like your earrings to match, record the distances between the holes.

6. Close the jump ring with pliers. Trim away the excess tape with scissors, leaving about 4 mm of tape beyond the last hole made.

7. Open the smaller silver jump ring, slip it through the larger jump ring, and close it. Open up the earring hook, slip it through the smaller jump ring, and close it.

8. Repeat steps 2 through 7 to make a second earring. The earrings don't have to match, so you can really be creative when making them!

→► Get Set

Drawing paper, acrylic paints (including metallics), and an old credit card or preprinted decorative papers

2 mini craft woodblocks, each 1.5 cm square

2 ear wires or hooks

Double-sided tape

Craft knife

Awl or sharp piercing tool

2 screw eyes, each 11 mm

Pliers

FINISHED SIZE
Each box, 1.5 cm square

→►► Go

1. Option: To create your own decorative papers, spread the acrylic paints onto the drawing paper, and smear or drag them around with the old credit card until the paper is covered. Add gold or metallic highlights to accentuate the design. Allow the paint to dry for five minutes.

2. Attach double-sided tape to the back of the decorative paper.

3. Select two wood blocks that are similar in size (these blocks can vary slightly). Set one block on top of the tape on the paper. Trim around the paper so it fits one surface of the block as closely as possible. Repeat this process to adhere paper to all surfaces of both blocks.

4. Decide which surface will be the top of each earring, making sure that both blocks look symmetrical when placed side by side. Pierce a small pilot hole in the center of the top of each block with an awl.

5. Insert a screw eye into each pilot hole, keeping it as straight as possible. The wood blocks are soft, so the screw eyes are usually easy to twist in by hand, but if they're tight, just use pliers to turn them gently.

6. Attach the earring hooks to the screw eyes.

Have Time to Spare?
Attach another screw eye to the bottom of each wood block. Then add beads, charms, or other decorative elements to further embellish the design.

Want to Make Another Pair?
Consider using new or vintage photographs in place of painted paper.

►► ► **Get Set**

12-karat gold-filled wire,
22 gauge, 30.5 cm

2 gold-filled ear wires
or posts and nuts

Bench tool kit, page 9

Fine point round-nose
pliers

FINISHED SIZE
Each, 2.5 x 1.9 cm

DESIGNER'S NOTE

Use the template below ❶
as a guide for bending
the wire. The instructions
start at the wrapped loop
and move toward the
porcupine's head.

►► ► **Go**

1. Using round-nose pliers, make a small
open loop, 6 mm from one end of the wire.
(You'll insert the earring post into this loop later.)

2. Starting at a point 8 mm from the loop,
bend 6-mm of the wire upward and the next
6 mm downward to make the first quill. Repeat
to make a second quill. Using the smooth
portion of the chain-nose pliers, squeeze the
tips of each quill tightly. (Note: Making these
quills uniform in size is easiest if you mark the
6 mm dimension on your plier jaws first, and
use the jaws to measure the wire.)

3. To create the porcupine's eye, 6 mm from
the base of the second quill, wrap the wire
around the very tip of the round-nose pliers.
To create the nose, make a sharp bend back
toward the body, 6 mm from the eye.

4. At a point 6 mm from the nose, bend the
wire away from the body to start the front leg.
Squeeze this bend tightly. To shape the foot,
make another sharp bend, 5 mm from the
first, and squeeze it tightly. The back of the
leg is 6 mm long.

5. The next 1.3 cm of wire forms the belly.
Round this section with your finger or with the
wide part of the round-nose pliers. At the end
of the belly, make a sharp forward bend to
start the back leg, and squeeze it tightly. The
front of this leg is 5 mm long. Make a second
bend to shape the foot, squeezing it tightly,
as well. The back of the leg, from the foot to
the tip of the tail, is 1.6 cm long.

6. To shape the tail, make a sharp bend
at its tip, and another 6 mm farther along.
Squeeze the tip of the tail tightly.

7. Shape each of the back quills by
repeating step 2 four times. Bend the wire
upward from the base of the last quill, and
squeeze the tips of each quill tightly.

8. Use the chain-nose pliers to make a
90-degree bend, 6 mm from the base of
the last quill. Beginning at this bend, wrap
the wire around the base of the open loop,
ending at the back. With the flush cutters,
clip off the excess from this end of the wire.
Bend the original end of the wire (below the
loop) up against the wraps, and cut it off
short and flush.

9. Repeat steps 1 through 8 to make the
second earring. Feed an ear wire or post
through the earring loop.

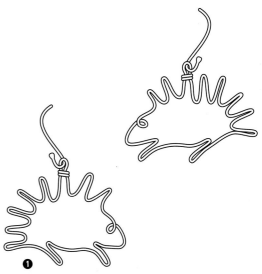

❶

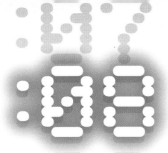

WIREWORK · FILING · HAMMERING

→► Get Set

Iron wire, 20 gauge,
   85½ inches (2.2 m)

Heavy-duty flush cutters

Metal file

Round-nose pliers

**Chain-nose or flat-nose
   pliers**

Utility hammer

Brass or steel wire brush

Wax sealant

FINISHED SIZE
Each hoop,
5.7 x 5.7 x 0.5 cm

→►► Go

1. Cut two 2¾-inch (7 cm) lengths of iron wire and set them aside. (You'll shape them into ear wires later.)

2. Cut the remaining iron wire in half. Each piece should be about 40 inches (101.6 cm) long. Set one piece aside.

3. File one end of the 40-inch (101.6 cm) wire smooth. Using round-nose pliers, bend 1 cm of the wire into a small loop.

4. Using your fingers, form the wire into a loose coil that measures approximately 2¼ inches (5.7 cm) in diameter. Include subtle corners and errant loops to achieve a look of controlled chaos. Continue until a total of six rounds have been formed, reserving about 1 to 1¼ inches (2.5 to 3.2 cm) of straight wire at the end.

5. Using chain-nose or flat-nose pliers, bend a right angle in the reserved wire, at the end of the last circle, then wrap the end of the wire two to three times around the circles to bind them together. Trim the end if necessary, then file it and tuck it into the wrapped circles.

6. Open the small wire loop made in step 3, and close it around an adjacent wire in the coil. (Note: Because the coil should be fairly flat, this is a good place to arrange and tuck in splaying wires.) Hammer the coil, being careful with areas where the wire overlaps.

7. To make the ear wires, file one end flat and form a small loop at the other end. Then bend the wire into a U shape at its center. Using chain-nose or flat-nose pliers, bend the filed end of the ear wire at an angle. Forge the angled end of the ear wire, file away any burrs, and hammer the central part of the wire.

8. Select a point on the coil to be the top of the hoop. Choose a wire from the six rounds at this point, and attach the ear-wire loop to it.

9. Repeat steps 3 through 8 to make the second earring. Clean the earrings with the wire brush and seal them with wax.

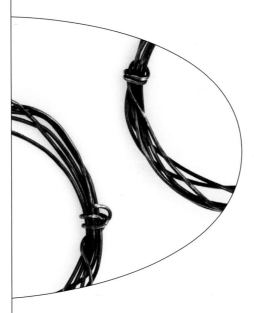

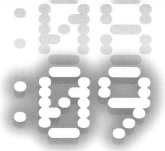

▶▶ Get Set

Covered button kit

2 fabric pieces, each
    2 x 2½ inches
    (5.1 x 6.4 cm)

2 fabric pieces, each
    1½ inches (3.8 cm)
    square

2 sterling silver or silver
    tone closed jump rings,
    each 5 mm

2 sterling silver or silver
    tone ear wires

Scissors

Needle

Thread, matching or
    complementary colors

Chain-nose pliers

FINISHED SIZE
Each, 5.1 x 2.9 x 0.8 cm

DESIGNER'S NOTES
Kits for making covered
buttons are available at
most fabric stores and
craft supply centers.

The fabric in this project
is a woven wool blend.

▶▶▶ Go

1. Following the button-kit instructions, make two 1⅛-inch (2.9 cm) and two ⅝-inch (1.6 cm) covered buttons. Hint: I like to use the tips of my scissors to gently coax the fabric so it catches on the teeth on the top part of the button.

2. Use a needle and thread to stitch a large button to a small button at their adjoining edges. Take care to hide the knots and clip the thread ends close; you shouldn't be able to see your stitches when you're finished. Repeat to attach the other two buttons.

3. Stitch a jump ring to the top edge of each small button. Be careful not to stitch too tightly, as this will cause the fabric to stretch and may cause it to tear. Hide the knots, and clip the thread ends close.

4. Using chain-nose pliers, open the ear wires just enough to slip the jump rings onto them. Gently close the findings with the pliers.

DESIGNERS: **BRYAN AND ANDREA RING**

DRILLING • SAWING • RIVETING
BENDING • WIREWORK

▶▶ ▶ Get Set

License plate

Sterling silver tubing,
  3 mm inside diameter

Sterling silver wire,
  20 gauge, approximately
  6 inches (15.2 cm)

Bench tool kit, page 9

FINISHED SIZE
Top pair:
Each, 3 x 1.4 x 1.5 cm

▶ ▶ ▶ Go

1. Mark two rectangles on the license plate, each 6 x 1.4 cm. Gradually taper and round the narrow ends of both rectangle drawings. (The shapes now resemble long ovals.)

2. Using a drill bit that corresponds to the outside diameter of the sterling silver tubing, drill a centered hole approximately 5 mm from each end of both metal shapes.

3. Cut out both drilled metal shapes, then file and sand their edges.

4. Measure the thickness of the license plate. Cut out four pieces of silver tubing, each 2 mm longer than the thickness of the license plate. Tube rivet all four drilled holes. (These rivets are decorative rather than functional.)

5. Bend each metal form into a hoop and align the riveted holes.

6. To make the ear wires, first cut the sterling silver wire in half. Feed one end of the wire through the aligned tube rivets, bend a neat loop, and wrap a tail of wire around the loop. Cut off any excess wire at the end of the wrapped loop. Bend the remaining wire into the ear hook. Repeat this process with the second earring and wire.

7. To finish the earrings, tap the ear wires with a hammer to work harden them.

Want to Make Another Pair?
Try these easy variations:
• Change the dimensions of the metal oval
• Join both drilled ends with one tube rivet

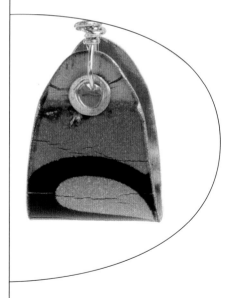

→ **Get Ready**

**SAWING • FILING • SANDING • POLISHING
TEXTURING • DRILLING • TWISTING**

→ ► **Get Set**

Sterling silver sheet,
  18 gauge, at least 1 x 4 cm

2 sterling silver ear wires

Bench tool kit, page 9

Hammer handpiece for
  flexible shaft fitted
  with diamond-tipped
  texturing tool or
  cylindrical diamond burr

2 pairs of parallel pliers
  with ends protected by
  tape or leather

FINISHED SIZE
Each, 5 x 0.5 x 0.5 cm

→ ► ► **Go**

1. Scribe two rectangles, each 4.5 x 40 mm, on the sterling silver sheet and cut them out. File 7 mm of each end into a long, tapered point with a rounded tip.

2. Sand the edges of the shapes with medium-grit and then fine-grit emery paper. Polish the fronts, backs, and edges.

3. Using the hammer handpiece fitted with a diamond-tipped texturing tool, evenly texture the entire front surfaces of both silver shapes. (Alternatively, use a cylindrical diamond burr and the flex shaft to apply an even texture.) Re-polish the back surfaces and edges if needed.

4. Mark a hole for the ear hooks near the top point of each silver shape, and drill the holes with a 0.8-mm drill bit.

5. Using the parallel pliers, grasp the top and bottom tapered sections of one of the silver shapes. Rotate the pliers in opposite directions until you've twisted the shape 360 degrees. Repeat with the second shape.

6. Attach the ear hooks to complete the earrings.

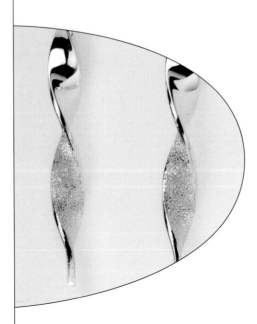

HAMMERING • WIREWORK • ADDING A PATINA (OPTIONAL)

▶▶ ▶ Get Set

2 copper washers, ¾ inch (1.9 cm) OD

2 sterling silver round wires, dead soft, 20 gauge, each 11.4 cm

2 ear wires

Bench tool kit, page 9

Liver of sulfur (optional)

Steel wool (optional)

FINISHED SIZE
Each, 2.2 x 2 x 0.2 cm

▶ ▶ ▶ Go

1. On a bench block or anvil, hammer a texture on one side of each washer using the ball end of a ball-peen hammer.

2. Straighten the two pieces of silver wire. Using round-nose pliers, bend each wire into an elongated U shape, with parallel "legs" of equal length that are approximately 4 mm apart.

3. Measure and mark each leg of a bent wire, 4 mm from the bend. Repeat with the other wire.

4. Grasp a wire with flat-nose pliers, just above the marks, and bend the legs up to form 90-degree angles.

5. Insert the wire ends through the center of a washer, from the back. Holding the washer with flat-nose pliers, carefully bend the wire ends and feed them through the hairpin loop.

6. Use the pliers to pull both wires tightly through the loop. Then bring each wire around the outside of the loop (on opposite sides) and back to the front of the washer. Trim both wires to 2.5 cm in length.

7. With round-nose pliers, form both wire ends into matching spirals, directing them away from the center of the earring. Then press the spirals down so that they rest on the front of the washer.

8. Repeat steps 4 through 7 to create the second earring.

9. On both earrings, attach an ear wire to the U-shaped loop in the silver wire.

10. To achieve an antique patina, dip the earrings in a warm liver of sulfur solution, rinse them in cold water, and buff them with steel wool.

VARIATION

13

→► Get Set

2 gold sheets, 14-karat,
    24 gauge, each
    5.4 x 2.2 cm

2 gold jump rings, 14-karat,
    22 or 20 gauge

2 gold ear wires, 14-karat

Bench tool kit, page 9

Photocopied design
    template ❶

FINISHED SIZE
Each, 4.5 x 2 x 0.5 cm

→►► Go

1. Cut out the photocopied design template. Glue or tape the two gold sheets together. (This allows you to cut out identical patterns at the same time.) Glue the template to the stacked gold sheets.

2. To remove the waste metal from the interior of each pattern, first create an indentation in that area with the center punch, and then drill a hole at this point for your saw blade. Saw out this interior area with the jeweler's saw. Then cut around the exterior lines of the pattern.

3. Remove any remaining glue or tape from the sawed metal shapes. File and slightly bevel all metal edges on both pieces.

4. Dome both ends of each metal shape in the dapping block. (Since there is a right and left earring, make sure they're domed on opposite sides.)

5. The narrow end of each metal form is threaded through the interior cutout in the wider end. Begin by using the half-round pliers to make a gentle bend in the narrowest, center area of the form. Then thread the narrow end through the cutout. Finish bending and shaping the metal with your fingers.

6. Add a jump ring and an ear wire to each earring. Polish both earrings.

❶
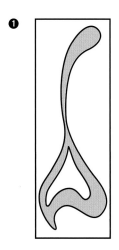

⮕ Get Ready

**SAWING • FILING • SANDING • POLISHING
DRILLING • BENDING • WIREWORK**

⮞▶ Get Set

Sterling silver sheet,
24 gauge, at least
3 x 4.2 cm

Round sterling silver wire,
20 gauge, 14.5 cm

4 sterling silver crimp
beads, to fit snugly on
the wire

Bicone crystal beads,
6 mm (6) and 4 mm (4)

Bench tool kit, page 9

FINISHED SIZE
Each, 3.7 x 1.4 x 1 cm

▶▶ Go

1. Scribe two 1.4 x 4.2-cm rectangles on the sterling silver sheet, and cut them out.

2. File and sand the edges of the rectangles, and polish all their surfaces.

3. Drill a hole near each end of both rectangles, 5 mm from the end and centered across the width.

4. Cover the front surfaces of the rectangles with tape to protect them. Then bend each piece over a cylindrical surface to form a gentle curve. Remove the protective tape and re-polish the pieces if necessary.

5. Re-drill the holes in each rectangle, using the same bit but angling the holes so that you'll be able to insert a silver wire through the top and bottom holes of each one without bending it (see step 8).

6. Cut the silver wire in half and straighten it if necessary. Sand and polish the ends of both pieces. Attach a crimp bead to the bottom of each wire by squeezing it tightly with chain-nose pliers.

7. Pass a wire up through the bottom hole of each rectangle, from the back, and string on the crystal beads, experimenting to achieve the look you want. Pass the wire through the top hole, string on another crimp bead, and crimp the bead in place against the back of each earring.

8. Using flat half-round pliers, bend the wires to fit through ear lobes, then bend the remaining length to follow the curve of the earring. If the wires are too long, cut them to the desired length, then round and polish their ends.

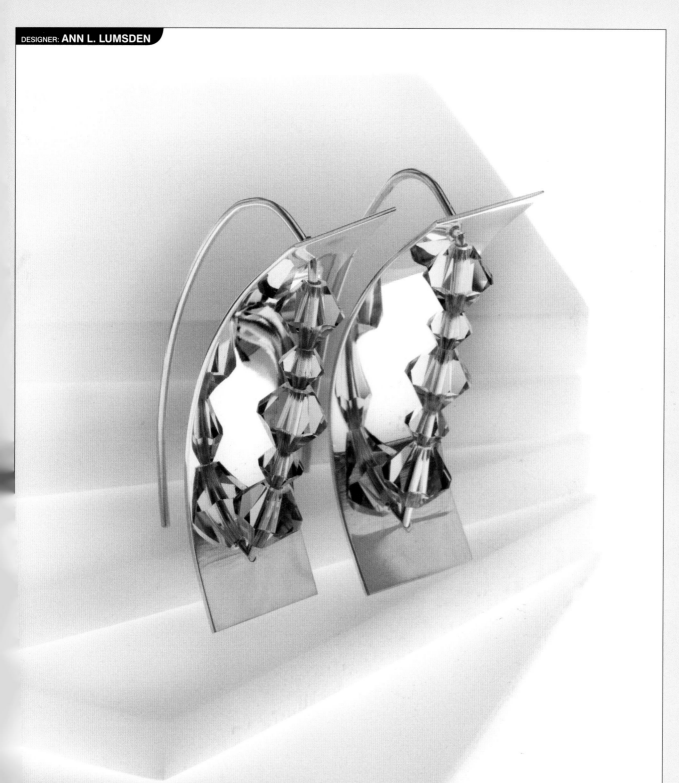

**SAWING · FILING · SANDING
DRILLING · DAPPING**

►► Get Set

2 round, half-drilled
   freshwater pearls,
   each 5 to 6 mm

Sterling silver sheet, dead
   soft, 28 gauge, 1½ x 2
   inches (3.8 x 5.1 cm)

2 sterling silver ear studs
   and nuts, 4-mm cups

Bench tool kit, page 9

Watchmaker's glue

Photocopied design
   template ❶

FINISHED SIZE
Each, 1 inch (2.5 cm)

►►► Go

1. Glue each of the half-drilled pearls onto the peg of an ear stud. Allow the glue to dry.

2. Using a scribe, transfer the photocopied flower template onto the sterling silver sheet two times.

3. Cut out the flower shapes with a jeweler's saw. File and sand all cut metal edges to clean and smooth them.

4. Create a subtle texture of radiating lines on each flower by running sandpaper from the center of the flower out to the tip of each petal.

5. Drill a hole in the center of each silver flower, making sure the hole is large enough to accommodate an ear stud.

6. Drill five additional decorative holes, one centered at the base of each flower petal (as shown on the design template). Sand the drilled holes smooth.

7. Place one silver flower in the center of the wooden dapping block. Using a dap and chasing hammer, depress the flower's central area so it's evenly concave. Repeat this step with the second flower.

8. Attach a pearl ear post to each silver flower by running it through the hole in the center of the flower.

Have Time to Spare?
Make these earrings super versatile by creating additional pearls studs in a range of sizes and colors to mix and match.

❶

**SAWING • POLISHING • ROLLER PRINTING • FILING
SANDING • DRILLING • WIREWORK**

▶ ▶ Get Set

Annealed sterling silver sheet, 24 gauge, large enough to accomodate four punched paper shapes (see step 2)

2 sterling silver ear wires

4 sterling silver jump rings, each 4 mm in diameter

Bench tool kit, page 9

Medium-sized paper punches (sun, flower, leaf, and snowflake designs)

Heavyweight paper

Clear tape

Rolling mill

Plastic template sheets, square and circle, approximately 1.7 cm

Steel burnisher (optional)

FINISHED SIZE
Each, 4.7 x 1.7 x 0.4 cm

DESIGNER'S NOTE
You may want to experiment rolling scrap silver sheet through the mill in order to determine the setting that will yield the desired result. Insufficient pressure will create a weak image, while too much pressure will distort the design.

▶ ▶ ▶ Go

1. Using the paper punches and heavyweight paper, punch out each of the four designs.

2. Scribe four squares onto the sterling silver sheet, making each one large enough to allow for a 3- to 4-mm margin on each side of the punched paper shapes. Cut out the squares and polish their front surfaces.

3. Center a punched paper design on the polished surface of each silver square, and place a plain piece of the same paper on the back surface, sandwiching the silver between the two pieces of paper. Protect the front surfaces of the silver squares by covering them with clear tape.

4. Roll each silver and paper stack through the mill. If necessary, flatten the rolled sheets by hand or with pliers with protected jaws.

5. Using the square and circle templates, mark a square on each silver sheet, and mark rounded tops on two of them. Cut out these shapes, and file and sand their edges. Use the steel burnisher to polish the edges if desired.

6. Using the project photo as a guide, mark and drill holes for the jump rings and ear hooks. Remove the protective tape, and attach the jump rings and hooks.

→ Get Ready

DRILLING • SAWING • FILING • FINISHING
WAXING (OPTIONAL)

►► Get Set

Sterling silver, copper,
   or brass sheet, 20 to 22
   gauge, 5.1 x 7.6 cm

Bench tool kit, page 9

2 photocopies of design
   template ❶

Rubber cement

3 radial bristle disks,
   400 grit

Wax sealant (optional)

FINISHED SIZE
Each, 6 x 0.7 x 2.1 cm

DESIGNER'S NOTES
Vary the drill bit diameters to
create graduated-size holes
in the earrings.

If you chose to use fine
silver, the thicker, 20-gauge
sheet is preferable.

►►► Go

1. Cut out the photocopied design templates, leaving at least ¼ inch (0.3 cm) of paper around each design.

2. Spread rubber cement on the backs of the templates and on the surface of the metal sheet. Let the adhesive set for a few seconds and then place the templates on the metal sheet, arranging them as close to each other as possible to reduce waste.

3. Using a center punch and chasing hammer, lightly dimple each mark for the drilled holes. Using a well-lubricated bit, drill holes at the dimples.

4. Cut out both earrings with the jeweler's saw. Remove all paper and rubber cement from the metal. File the edges of the earrings smooth and deburr the drilled holes, if necessary.

5. With the bristle disk attachments turning at medium speed, gently go over the earrings in one direction, rounding out the curved edges first and then running over the other surfaces.

6. Using a kitchen scrub pad and dish soap, wash the earrings to remove any sanding dust, dirt, or oil from fingers. Dry the earrings.

7. Optional: Warm a tiny bit of wax sealant with your fingers and spread it in a thin, even coat over all earring surfaces. Set the earrings aside to dry for a couple of minutes before buffing them with a clean rag.

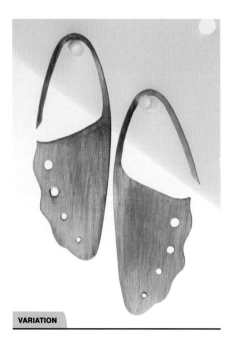

VARIATION

❶

**BASIC METAL CLAY WORK • DRILLING • MELTING WIRE ENDS
DAPPING • FINISHING • WIREWORK**

►► Get Set

2 packets of square silver
   clay sheet

Copper sheet, 28 gauge,
   7.6 cm square

2 round sterling silver
   wires, 20 gauge, each
   9 cm long

Bench tool kit, page 9

Soldering kit, page 9

Programmable kiln suitable
   for firing metal clay, with
   kiln shelf

Flower-shaped paper
   punches in 3 sizes

Kiln fork

Brass bristle wheel

Round-hole drawplate
   and flat steel hammer
   (optional)

Knitting needle

FINISHED SIZE
Each, 5.4 x 3.5 x 1.5 cm

►►► Go

1. Preheat the kiln to 1650°F (900°C) and set it to hold for 15 minutes. Open the packets of metal clay sheet. Use the paper punches to punch out six flowers from the sheets, two in each of the three sizes. Place the six flowers on the kiln shelf. Use the kiln fork to place the shelf carefully in the kiln. Shut the door quickly to avoid heat loss. Keep an eye on the kiln and the time. The flowers need a minimum of 10 minutes at 1650°F (900°C).

2. Use the paper punches to punch out six flowers from the 28-gauge copper sheet, two in each of the three sizes. Mark the center of each copper flower with the center punch, and drill holes through those points with a 0.9-mm drill bit.

3. Use a torch to melt a ball on one end of each 20-gauge sterling silver wire. Pickle and rinse the balled wires. Shine the wires with a brass bristle brush and soapy water, and then rinse and dry them. Optional: To flatten the balls on the wire ends, thread one wire through the 0.8-mm hole in a drawplate until the ball is flush with the front part of the plate. Use a flat steel hammer to tap the ball into a flat round. Repeat with the other wire.

4. Once the metal clay flowers have fired for 10 minutes, carefully remove the hot kiln shelf with the kiln fork and place it on a heatproof surface close to the kiln. Pick up the hot metal flowers with tweezers and quench then in water. Dry the flowers well.

5. Mark the center of each silver flower with the center punch, and drill holes at those points with the 0.9-mm bit. (This only takes a few seconds by hand, as the metal is so thin.)

6. To make the earrings, stack the silver and copper flowers in alternating layers of graduated sizes, with the largest flowers on the bottom. (Because metal clay slightly shrinks when fired, each stack will have six different sizes of flowers.)

7. Place a set of stacked flowers into a wide dapping block, with the largest flower on the bottom. Press down on the stack with a large doming punch to give the flowers a gentle curve. (There's no need to use a hammer, as the thin metal bends very easily.) Repeat with the other stack.

8. Thread an earring wire through the holes in one stack so that the ball rests at the front. Push the ball against the smallest flower, and hold it in place with your thumb. With your other hand, bend the wire up at a 90° angle, as close to the back of the stacked flowers as possible. Repeat to attach a wire to the other earring.

9. Dip each earring into soapy water. Then, using a small brass bristle wheel and flex shaft, flick over the surface of each wet flower for a few seconds, inside and out. Be careful not to catch the edges of the flower, or you'll bend them.

10. To shape the wires into matching hooks, bend one over a knitting needle to form an arch. Leave this earring on the needle as you bend the other wire next to it. Using half-round pliers, shape a series of gentle curves in each ear wire. If needed, snip the wires to matching lengths. File and sand the ends of the wires so they'll slide comfortably through your ear lobes.

**DRILLING • SAWING • FILING • STONE SETTING
SANDING • WIREWORK**

►► Get Set

2 square sterling silver
  wires, 10 gauge, each
  1 inch (2.5 cm)

2 round faceted stones,
  each 3 mm

2 sterling silver fish-hook
  ear wires, 20 gauge

Bench tool kit, page 9

Piece of scrap copper
  sheet (optional)

Hart burr, 3 mm

FINISHED SIZE
Each, 3.6 x 0.6 x 0.4 cm

►►► Go

1. Using a center punch and hammer, mark the metal on one face of one wire, about 2 mm from the top. With the flex shaft and a 1-mm bit, drill a hole straight through the square wire. Repeat this step, and all the following steps, to create the second earring at the same time.

2. On the same face as the drilled hole but at the opposite end, measure up about 7 mm from the bottom of the wire. Use dividers to mark a line from that point, down the middle of the wire to the bottom.

3. Using a jeweler's saw, cut straight along the marked line. Separate the cut square wire into two sections, forming a V shape. (Tip: Inserting a small piece of thin copper into the cut is the easiest way to start separating the metal. This also prevents marking the metal.)

4. Gently file the inner surfaces of the V cut with a barrette needle file to smooth out any saw marks. With the same file, smooth the blunt edges at the ends of the V by filing them at slight angles.

5. For the earring to hang properly, the top end of the square wire needs thinning. To do this, use a flat file to create slopes on both drilled faces by filing them at an angle. When the metal is thin enough, smooth out the top edge with a barrette needle file.

6. To create the seat for the stone, use the flex shaft and hart burr. Position the burr slightly more than halfway up the interior of the inverted V and a little towards the front of the earring. (You may need to slightly close the V with flat pliers so that the metal surfaces meet the burr.) Push the burr into the top of the narrowed V to form the seat.

7. Set the stone into the grooves with its table (flat face) facing out, and carefully close the V with flat pliers. Check to make sure that the stone is immobile and secure within the seat.

8. Using emery paper, sand all the outer metal surfaces in the same direction until the finish is even and matte.

9. Using round-nose pliers, carefully uncurl the loop at the bottom of the ear wire, slip the end through the hole at the top of the earring (making sure the proper stone surface is facing forward), and loop the wire back around the top of the earring. You may need to adjust the loop to ensure that the earring hangs freely from the ear wire.

DESIGNER: **ELLEN HIMIC**

→ Get Ready

►► Get Set

Rubber sheet, 2 mm thick, color of your choice

Silver sheet, 20 gauge, 4 x 1.5 cm

16 silver tube beads, 2 mm in diameter and length

2 silver wires, 18 gauge, each 7.6 cm

2 half-drilled freshwater pearls

Bench tool kit, page 9

Disk cutter

Sewing needle

Five-minute epoxy

Crimping pliers

FINISHED SIZE
Each, 5.1 x 2 x 1.2 cm

TIME SAVER
Purchase readymade silver and rubber disks and you won't have to spend any time punching your own!

►►► Go

1. Using the disk cutter, punch out various sizes of circles from the rubber and silver sheets. In this project, each earring features: 2 small rubber disks (0.6 cm); 2 large rubber disks (1.1 cm); 2 small silver disks (1 cm); and 1 large silver disk (1.3 cm).

2. Sand the edges of the silver disks smooth. Drill a hole through the center of each silver disk and smooth away any burrs.

3. Use a sewing needle to make a hole in the center of each rubber disk.

4. Feed the tube beads onto the 18-gauge wires, alternating them with the rubber and silver disks. (In the earrings pictured, the disks are fed in this order, each separated by tube beads: small rubber, small silver, large rubber, large silver, large rubber, small silver, small rubber.)

5. Using the five-minute epoxy, glue a half-drilled pearl onto the wire at the bottom of each earring. Let dry.

6. Slide the beads and discs down each wire to meet the pearl. Crimp the tube bead at the top of each stack with crimping pliers.

7. Shape the upper end of each wire into an ear hook with round needle-nose pliers.

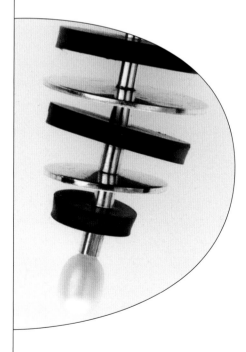

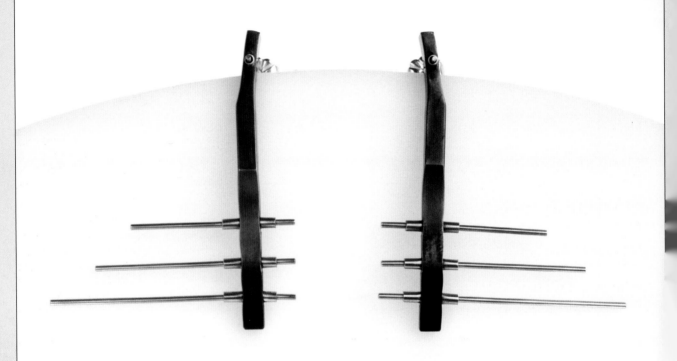

Get Ready

**SAWING • FILING • SANDING • DRILLING
USING A ROLLING MILL • FINISHING**

▶ ▶ Get Set

Sterling silver wire,
    18 gauge, 14 inches
    (35.6 cm)

2 square brass rods,
    8 gauge, each 1½
    inches (3.8 cm)

Sterling silver tube, 1.6 mm
    OD, 1 mm ID, 3 inches
    (7.6 cm)

2 earring posts and nuts

Bench tool kit, page 9

Table vise

Draw tongs or vise-grip
    pliers

Conical burr (setting
    burr or hart burr),
    approximately 2 mm

Patina for brass (optional)

Steel wool (optional)

Rolling mill

FINISHED SIZE
Each, 4.5 x 4 x 1.6 cm

▶ ▶ ▶ Go

1. To stretch, straighten, and temper the silver wire, and reduce its diameter, tighten one end in the table vise, grasp the other end with draw tongs or vise-grip pliers, and pull the wire straight toward you. Cut the straightened silver wire into six pieces: two 1½ inches (3.8 cm) long; two 1¼ inches (3.2 cm) long; and two 1 inch (2.5 cm) long.

2. Deburr the ends of the brass pieces with a flat file and sand them with emery paper to create a smooth finish.

3. Cut the silver tube into six ⅜-inch-long (1 cm) and two ³⁄₁₆-inch-long (0.5 cm) pieces. Smooth and deburr the edges with a file. Use the conical burr to deburr the interior of each tube.

4. Choose one flat surface on each brass rod piece, and measure and mark points that are 4 mm, 8 mm, and 12 mm up from the bottom. Use a center punch to make a divot at each marked point.

5. Rotate each brass rod piece 90 degrees so that a flat surface adjacent to the divoted one is face up. Measure, mark, and divot each piece, 4 mm down from the top. Each brass piece should now have a mark on one flat surface, near one end, and three marks on an adjacent surface, at the other end. Using a 1.6-mm bit, drill four holes through each brass piece, one at each divot. Deburr the drilled holes.

6. Polish the silver with a polishing cloth. Finish the brass as desired: polish it, use steel wool for a matte finish, sandblast it, or add an oxide patina.

7. Insert one of the longest silver wires into a long tube. Carefully push this assembly into the lowest of the three holes in the brass rod. Push a medium-length silver wire into a long tube, and insert that into the middle hole. Finally, push one of the shortest wires into the remaining long tube, and insert the tube into the uppermost hole. Center the tubes in the holes, and align the wire ends evenly on one side, as shown in the project photo. Repeat this step with the other wires, tubes, and rod.

8. Open the rolling mill rollers to accommodate the thickness of one brass rod. Insert the bottom of the rod—the end with the silver inserts—into the roller. Tighten the tension wheel on the roller one-half turn. Check the earring assembly to make sure nothing is out of position, then slowly force about 2 cm of the rod through the roller, passing the silver inserts. Back the assembly out and inspect it for alignment. Repeat this process several times, gradually tightening the roller tension each time in small increments, until all three silver components are firmly held in place by pressure and no longer move when pulled. Repeat this step with the other assembled earring.

9. Insert an earring post into each of the shortest silver tubes, and insert the tubes into the holes at the top of each earring. Run this end of each earring through the roller, as you did in step 8, but only roll 1 cm of the rod's length, just past the ear post-and-tube assembly. Wipe the earrings clean or apply a patina to the brass or silver or to both.

⮞ Get Ready

⮞⮞ Get Set

Copper sheet, 2 gauge,
    3-inch (7.6 cm) square

2 sterling silver French
    ear wires

Bench tool kit, page 9

Soldering kit, page 9

Fine steel wool

Circle punch, 1¼ inches
    (3.2 cm) in diameter

Sanding stick

Stamping tool

Patina solution, to color
    copper without coloring
    silver

FINISHED SIZE
Each, 5 x 3.2 cm

DESIGNER'S NOTE
Instead of stamping, you
can use a rolling mill to
create a texture or buy
patterned sheet.

⮞⮞⮞ Go

1. Rub the steel wool over both sides of the copper sheet. Using the circle punch, cut out two circles from the sheet, each 1¼ inches (3.2 cm) in diameter. File the edges of both circles with the metal file, and sand them with the sanding stick.

2. Stamp a design on each circle, using a stamping tool and hammer. Either choose a deep design or hammer heavily. (For this project, the copper circles were entirely covered with randomly placed designs.)

3. Place one stamped copper circle right side up on the charcoal block, and flux it. Place wire solder in locking tweezers. Heat the copper to flow temperature, and rub the wire solder over the copper to flow the solder. Continue until the entire piece is covered with solder. If necessary, use a pick to move

the solder. Repeat this step with the second copper circle. Pickle, rinse, and dry both circles.

4. Carefully file the solder off each circle until the pattern is revealed, and stop filing as soon as you see the pattern. Then, sand the circles with the sanding stick. (Don't sand too much or you'll remove your pattern!)

5. Determine the top of each earring and drill a hole that is 2 mm inside the edge. Sand the burrs off after drilling.

6. Dome the earrings in a dapping block.

7. Following the manufacturer's instructions, add a patina to the earrings. Insert the ear wires through the drilled holes.

Want to Make Another Pair?
Mix up your metals! Make these earrings with sterling silver sheet and gold solder or with gold sheet and sterling silver solder.

→ Get Ready

GLUING • VARNISHING • SAWING • DRILLING • DAPPING • FILING
SANDING • MELTING WIRE ENDS (OPTIONAL) • WIREWORK

▶▶ **Get Set**

Page from a book

Silver sheet, 22 gauge

2 silver wires, 22 gauge,
    each 8 cm

2 silver ear wires

Bench tool kit, page 9

Soldering kit, page 9
    (optional)

Glue

Stain or paraffin

Small paintbrush

FINISHED SIZE
Each, 4.2 x 0.8 x 0.8 cm

▶▶▶ **Go**

1. Cut two strips of paper from the page of a book, each 3 x 18 cm. Roll up each strip, and glue down its end.

2. Varnish the paper rolls by applying stain or paraffin with a small paintbrush. Let dry.

3. Saw out six circles from the silver sheet, each 9 mm in diameter (or use a disk cutter).

4. In the center of each circle, make an indentation with the center punch. Using a 0.8-mm bit, drill holes through the indentations.

5. Using a dapping block and punches, dome the metal circles. Re-drill the center holes on the domes. File and sand the edges to finish them.

6. To make a small ball on one end of each piece of silver wire, start by grasping the wire with tweezers and fluxing one end. Then hold the wire upside down, and heat it from underneath with a torch. (If you don't have a soldering torch, just round the wire ends with round-nose pliers.)

7. Cut each wire to 4.5 cm in length. Use files and sandpaper to finish the surfaces of the balled wire.

8. To assemble each earring, thread a wire through a domed circle (convex surface face down), a paper roll, and two more domed circles—the first with its convex surface facing up, and the other with that surface facing down. Using round-nose pliers, form the upper end of the wire into a loop, and insert an ear wire through the loop.

DESIGNER: **DOROTHEA HOSOM**

 **24**

→ Get Ready

SAWING · FILING · SANDING · DRILLING · WIREWORK

►► ► **Get Set**

Compact disc jewel case, black plastic

Steel wire, 22 gauge, 5 cm

2 gunmetal ear wires

Bench tool kit, page 9

Tweezers

Gun blue for steel

Household glue

Acrylic satin varnish (optional)

Colored metal foil (optional)

FINISHED SIZE
Each, 3.8 x 1.7 x 1.7 cm

DESIGNER'S NOTE
Steel wire and gun blue are available at many hardware stores. Beading stores and jewelry suppliers sell the ear wires, and crafts shops often carry colored metal foil.

►► ► **Go**

1. Using a scribe, mark four circles on the CD jewel case, each 1.7 cm in diameter.

2. Cut out the circles with a jeweler's saw, and then lightly file and sand all edges. Mark a center line through each circle.

3. On each circle, measure, mark, and cut out a slot that is 9 mm long and 1 mm wide. The slot runs from the edge of the circle to its center.

4. Fit the slots of the circles together in pairs to make two earrings.

5. At the top of each earring, drill a hole on the thin edge of the intersecting circles.

6. Cut the 22-gauge wire in half. With round-nose pliers, form one end of each wire into a small loop.

7. Grip each wire with tweezers and dip it into the gun blue. Rinse the wires immediately and wipe them off with a paper towel.

8. Apply a very small amount of glue to the straight end of each wire, and insert that end into the drilled hole at the top of the earrings. Attach the gunmetal ear wires or ear wires of your choice to the loops.

Have Time to Spare?
Brush the plastic surfaces of the earrings with acrylic satin varnish and cover them with metal foil. Apply another coat or two of varnish and dry thoroughly.

25

➤ Get Ready

WIREWORK • SAWING • FILING • CHASING • DRILLING DAPPING • FINISHING • ADDING HEAT PATINA

➤➤ Get Set

Titanium wire, 18 gauge, 38 cm long

Sterling silver sheet, 20 gauge

2 silver jump rings, 0.7 cm in diameter

2 silver ear wires

Bench tool kit, page 9

Soldering kit, page 9

Photocopied flower templates ❶

Bracelet or round mandrel, approximately 5 cm in diameter

Rotary tumbler

Chasing liner tool

FINISHED SIZE
Each, 9.5 x 5.5 x 1.9 cm

DESIGNER'S NOTE
If you've never colored titanium before, practice step 8 on a flat piece of titanium before attempting this project.

➤➤➤ Go

1. To create one double-circle hoop for each earring, wrap the titanium wire twice around the mandrel, and tap it with a rawhide mallet. (Titanium is very hard and tends to spring back to its original shape, so you may want to start by wrapping the wire around a small-diameter section of the mandrel; then slowly enlarge the hoops by moving the wire toward the base.)

2. Place the shaped wires in a tumbler for five minutes to change their matte gray color to a more vibrant gray. (Polished titanium colors faster and offers more vibrant colors than unpolished titanium.)

3. Adhere the photocopied flower templates to the sterling silver sheet. Saw the shapes from the metal and file their edges to give them a clean look.

4. One at a time, place the silver flowers on the bench block and use a chasing liner tool and hammer to indent the straight lines that separate the petals. Note: Make sure your punch is polished so that it won't leave any unnecessary marks on the flower.

5. Drill two holes in each flower, side by side and as close to the flower centers as possible. Start with a 0.8-mm drill bit and gradually enlarge each hole, moving up to a 1.1-mm bit.

6. Slightly dome each flower in the dapping block. Because the flowers are already slightly concave, a single strike of the hammer will be enough to achieve the desired effect. Create a matte finish on both silver flowers with a kitchen scrub pad.

7. To create a "third-hand" that will hold the hoops as you apply heat to color them, bend one end of a length of titanium wire into a fishhook shape, and insert the other end into a soldering block. Suspend one of the shaped hoops from the bent end of the wire.

8. Light your torch and adjust the flame to one that is large and soft—the one that occurs at the stage right before the transparent blue annealing flame. Move this flame gradually around the hoops, evenly and in a clockwise direction, until the color starts to appear in the metal. (The colors appear in the following order: yellow, purple, blue, and gray.) Stop once you've achieved the color you desire. Repeat to color the other set of hoops and allow the colored metal to cool.

9. Thread each hoop wire through the two holes in a flower. Use round-nose pliers to turn small, closed loops at the ends of both wire hoops. Open a jump ring and feed it through both loops in a hoop wire. Repeat with the other jump ring and hoop wire. Slide the ear wires through the jump rings.

❶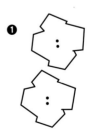

DESIGNER: **MELISSA MUIR**

► Get Ready

TEXTURING (OPTIONAL) • USING A DISK CUTTER • DRILLING
ANNEALING • DAPPING • SOLDERING • WIREWORK
HAMMERING • FILING • POLISHING

►► Get Set

Sterling silver sheet, dead soft, 24 gauge, 2 inches (5.1 cm) square

Copper sheet, 26 gauge, 1 x 2 inches (2.5 x 5.1 cm)

Sterling silver round wire, dead soft, 20 gauge, 7 inches (17.8 cm)

Bench tool kit, page 9

Soldering kit, page 9

Disk cutter

Heavy brass mallet

Planishing hammer

Radial bristle sanding disks

Tumbler with stainless steel media

Patina (optional)

FINISHED SIZE
Each, 5 x 1.5 x 1 cm

►►► Go

1. Texture one or both of the sheet metals if desired, and then clean them completely. Using the disk cutter and heavy brass mallet, cut out two ⅝-inch (1.9 cm) silver disks and two ⁵⁄₁₆-inch (0.8 cm) copper disks.

2. Drill a small hole through the center of each silver disk. Anneal and pickle all four metal disks. Using a dapping block and punch set, slightly dome each disk.

3. Coat all the disks with a thin layer of paste flux. Place the silver disks on your soldering surface, with their concave surfaces facing up. Place a copper disk inside each silver disk, with its concave surface facing the same direction. Cut small, 1-mm squares of hard sheet solder and place them on the soldering surface, near the disks. With the torch, warm the solder chips until they ball up.

4. Warm the undersides of the outer disks until the flux turns from a powdery white to a brown syrup consistency. With a soldering pick or sharp tweezers, place two small balls of solder on the seam where each pair of nested disks meets. Continue to warm the disks evenly, concentrating on the seam from underneath, until the solder has flowed around the seam. Pickle the soldered disks and dry them well.

5. Cut the sterling silver wire into two 3 ½-inch-long (8.9 cm) pieces to use as ear wires. Using a planishing hammer and steel block, slightly flatten about ⅛-inch (0.3 cm) on one end of each wire, and touch up any rough edges with a needle file.

6. Flux the disks and wires and place them on the soldering surface, with the silver domes facing up. Using the third hand to hold the flattened end of the ear wire against the back of the domed disk, solder each wire in place with easy solder. Pickle the earrings and dry them well. Remove any excess solder with a sanding disk.

7. Form the ear wires by bending each one into a U shape around the tips of your round-nose pliers, about 1½ (3.8 cm) inches from the tops of the domed disks. Use the flat-nose pliers to ensure that the area of each wire that's closest to the disks is straight. Then use your thumb and forefinger to make a gentle curve in the rest of each wire. The ear wires should look somewhat like incomplete capital letters D when viewed from the side.

8. Round the ends of the ear wires with a file, and sandpaper or a cup burr. Place the earrings in a tumbler with stainless steel shot and burnishing liquid to harden and polish them. Apply any desired patina.

Want to Make Another Pair?
Here are two variations to explore:
• Vary the disk diameters
• Change the direction of the domes

➤ Get Ready

**SOLDERING • FORGING • SANDING
DRILLING • WIREWORK**

➤ ▶ Get Set

2 sterling silver jump rings, 16 gauge, each 1.3 to 1.4 cm in diameter

2 round sterling silver wires, 20 gauge, 6.4 cm

2 coin pearls, each 12 to 13 mm

Bench tool kit, page 9

Soldering kit, page 9

Metal ring mandrel

Ring clamp

Sanding stick

Bracelet pliers or mandrel

FINISHED SIZE
Each, 4.4 x 1.9 cm

▶ ▶ ▶ Go

1. Solder the jump rings closed; then pickle, rinse, and dry them.

2. Using a fine-tipped marker, mark the solder joint on each jump ring, and mark the spot that is exactly opposite it, across the diameter of the ring.

3. Place a jump ring on the mandrel, with one marked spot on top. Forge that spot until it's flat and wide enough to accommodate a drill bit. Repeat at the second marked point and at both points on the other jump ring.

4. To flatten the two outer areas of each ring, place the ring in the ring clamp, position it so half of the ring is on the bench block, and hammer. Keep your hands and fingers off the bench block as you do this, move the ring from left to right, and keep your hammer blows light and even. To give the flattened

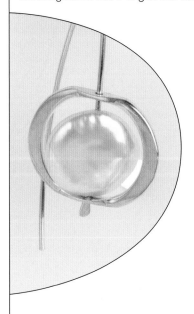

area a graduated look, spend more time hammering its middle. Repeat this process on the opposite side of the ring, and on both sides of the second jump ring.

5. Use a sanding stick to sand out any rough hammer marks on both rings.

6. Mark and drill holes at the top and bottom of each ring. Sand away any burrs, and finish the rings as desired.

7. Sand and round both ends of each piece of 20-gauge wire. Holding a wire just on the edge of the bench block, hammer one end flat. Repeat to flatten one end of the other wire.

8. To assemble each earring, thread the round end of a wire through one hole in a ring, through a pearl, and then through the other hole in the ring. Push the ring to the flattened bottom of the wire.

9. Using bracelet pliers or a mandrel, start to form both wires, going over them several times to harden them. (If you use a mandrel, planish the wires to harden them.)

10. Make a mark on each wire, ¾ inch (1.9 cm) from the top of the ring. Using round-nose pliers, bend the wires back at this point to form ear wires.

Want to Make Another Pair?
• Try using differently shaped beads. Adjust the size of the ring to accommodate the bead.
• Make two or three types of rings that fit inside one another and twirl.

Get Ready

SANDING • POLISHING • DRILLING
SOLDERING (OPTIONAL) • WIREWORK

► Get Set

2 strips of sterling silver sheet, 30 or 32 gauge, each 27 x 0.5 cm

2 strips of paper, each 27 x 0.5 cm

2 round silver wires, 22 or 24 gauge, each 20 cm

8 sterling silver crimp beads

2 pearls, 7 mm

Bench tool kit, page 9

Soldering kit, page 9 (optional)

Tape

Large can or mandrel

Crimping pliers

FINISHED SIZE
Each, 9.5 x 3 x 0.3 cm

► ► ► Go

1. Sand and polish the two sterling silver strips.

2. Fold the paper strips into random lengths, positioning the folds in a way that will allow you to drill a hole through each fold. Open each folded paper strip, and copy the location of the folds onto the sterling silver strips with a marker.

3. Fold the sterling silver strips at the marked points. With tape, bind the folded metal pieces onto a wooden block. Drill a hole through the center of each folded piece.

4. If the two sterling silver wires aren't already slightly curved, gently bend them over a large can or mandrel.

5. If soldering: Cut a 15-cm and 5-cm length from each piece of wire. Solder each shorter wire to a longer one at a 30-degree angle. If not soldering: Measure 5 cm in from one end, and bend the wires at a 30-degree angle.

6. String a crimp bead onto each 15-cm wire and squeeze the bead closed about 3 cm from the soldered or bent corner.

7. Remove the tape from the pieces of folded silver. Thread the longer wire section through the drilled holes in each piece. Using the project photo as a guide, carefully unfold the strips and slide a few of the folds off the wire to make a space for the pearl.

8. Thread a crimp bead, a pearl, and a second crimp bead onto each long wire. Push the upper portion of each strip up to the squeezed crimp bead before rethreading the wire through the rest of the folded strip.

9. Secure both silver strips by squeezing a crimp bead at the bottom of each one.

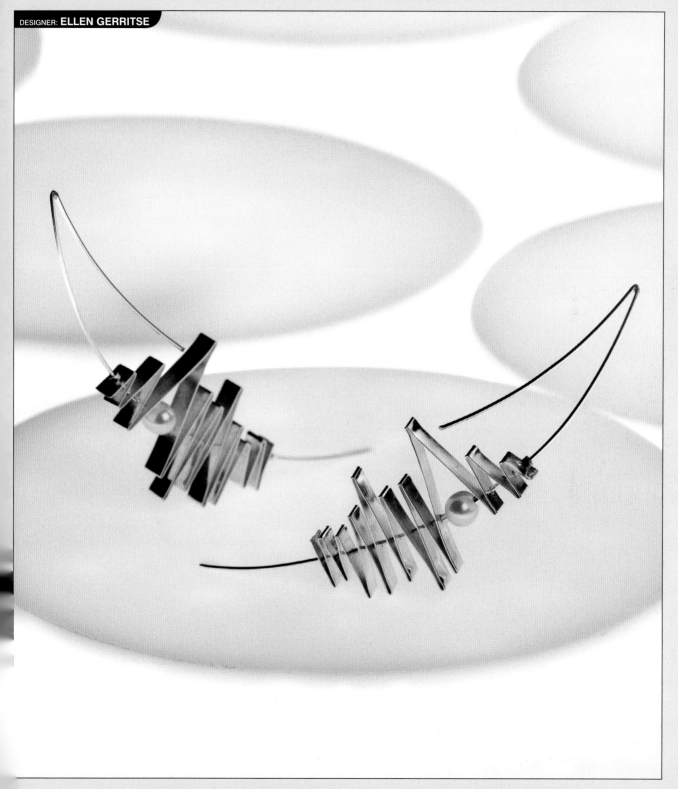

DESIGNER: **SIM LUTTIN**

► Get Ready

MELTING WIRE ENDS • HAMMERING • DRILLING • SANDING
ADDING A PATINA • SEALING • WIREWORK

►► Get Set

2 fine silver wires,
   18 gauge, each 2 cm

28 sterling silver wires,
   15 gauge, each
   1.3 cm long

2 sterling silver ear wires

Bench tool kit, page 9

Soldering kit, page 9

Liver of sulfur solution

Beeswax or wax polish
   for metal

FINISHED SIZE
Each, 3.8 x 0.8 x 0.8 cm

►►► Go

1. Using a torch, heat one end of each of the 2-cm-long fine silver wires until a small ball forms, approximately 1 mm in diameter. Set the two wires aside.

2. With the forging hammer, strike once across the center of each 1.3-cm long sterling silver wire to indent and bend it. Then drill a hole in the center of each indentation. Sand off any burrs.

3. Place the drilled silver wires in the liver of sulfur solution and check them at 10-second intervals. Once the wires are thoroughly blackened, rinse the pieces in cold water, and then polish and seal them with wax.

4. Thread 14 of the blackened silver wires onto each length of the fine silver wire. Make a slightly open loop at the top of each fine silver wire with round-nose pliers to secure the blackened elements.

5. Slide the loop at the top of each earring onto the loop of an ear wire, and then close the loops to secure.

▶ ▶ **Get Set**

Round sterling silver wire, 20 gauge, 5 cm long

Round sterling silver wire, 22 gauge, 90 cm long

2 ear nuts

Bench tool kit, page 9

Soldering kit, page 9

Cup burr

Tumbler (optional)

FINISHED SIZE
Each, 6.7 x 1 x 1.5 cm

▶ ▶ ▶ **Go**

1. Cut the 20-gauge sterling silver wire in half to make two 2.5-cm lengths.

2. To form the earring posts, use flat-nose and round-nose pliers to bend a 3- to 4-mm ring at one end of each 20-gauge wire piece.

3. Solder the rings at the end of the earring posts closed, and then pickle both posts.

4. Cut the 22-gauge sterling silver wire into six pieces, each 15 cm long.

5. Run one length of the 22-gauge sterling silver wire through the ring at the end of one earring post. Fold the wire in half, and twist its ends together with flat-nose pliers. Repeat this process to add two more wires to the same ear post.

6. Repeat step 5 with the remaining 22-gauge wires on the second ear post, folding the wires in half and twisting their ends.

7. Secure one set of twisted wire ends in the chuck of the flexible shaft, and twist the folded wires together. Repeat this process for each folded wire on both ear posts.

8. Trim each earring post to 1 cm in length.

9. Using a cup burr attachment on the flexible shaft, round the ends of the earring posts.

10. With a torch, melt the ends of each twisted wire to form a ball. Pickle the earrings and finish them in a tumbler if desired.

Have Time to Spare?
These earrings also look great when oxidized.

DESIGNER: **RAÏSSA BUMP**

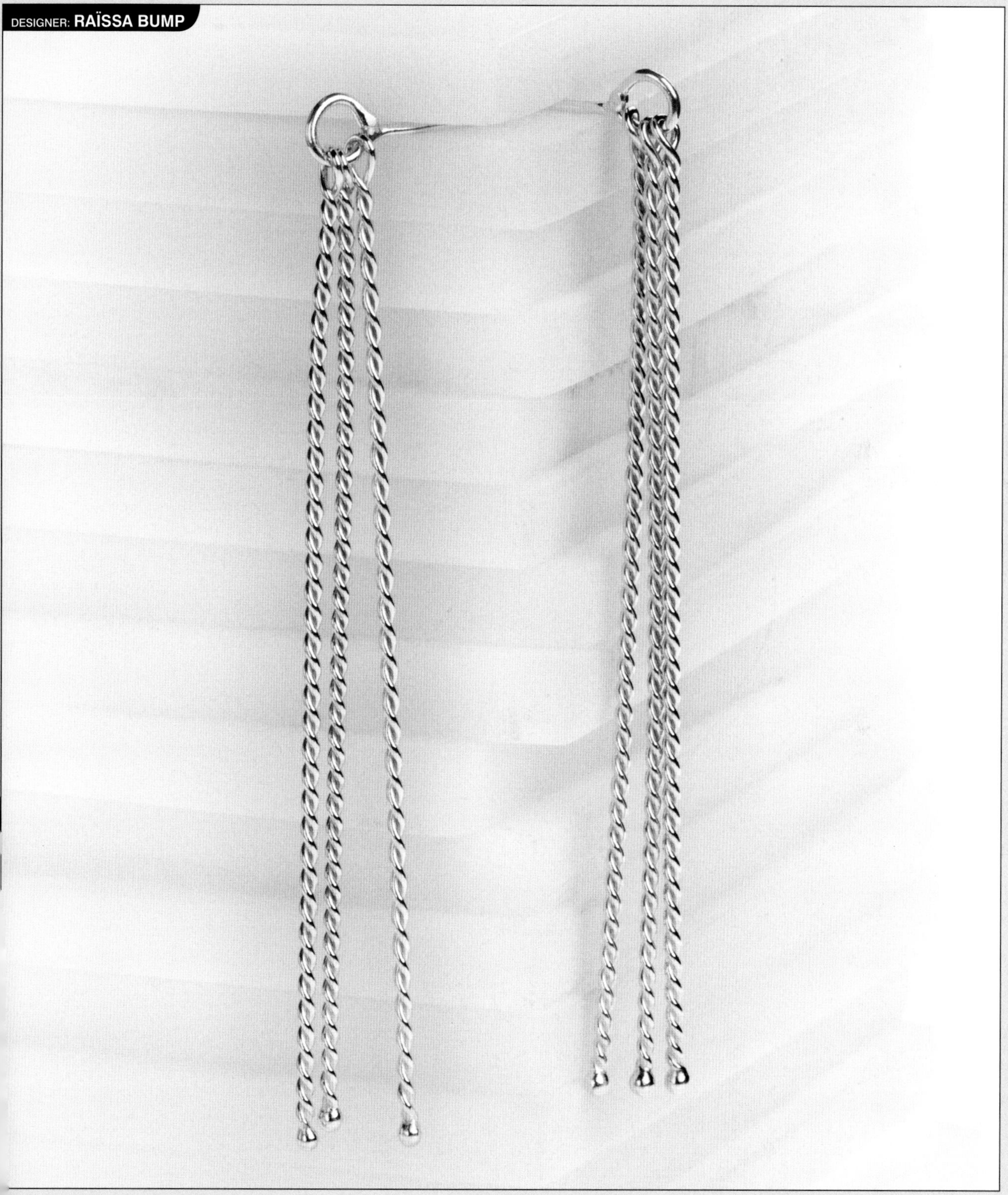

→ Get Ready

SAWING • HAMMERING • FILING • SANDING • DRILLING SOLDERING • WIREWORK • POLISHING

►► Get Set

Round sterling silver wire,
   16 gauge, 30 cm

Round sterling silver wire,
   20 gauge, 4 cm

2 earring nuts

Bench tool kit, page 9

Soldering kit, page 9

Ring clamp or vise

FINISHED SIZE
Each, 4 cm in diameter

►►► Go

1. Cut both the 16-gauge and the 20-gauge sterling silver wires in half.

2. Place one piece of the 16-gauge wire on a steel block, and hammer the tip of one end to flatten it. File and sand both ends of this wire to round and smooth them.

3. Use a center punch to make a divot in the non-flattened end of the wire. Clamp the wire in the ring clamp or vise, and drill a 2-mm-deep hole at the divot. Sand off any burrs that formed during drilling.

4. Sand and flux the drilled wire and one piece of the 20-gauge wire (the ear wire). Fit the ear wire into the hole in the 16-gauge wire, and solder the wires together. Pickle, rinse, and dry the soldered pieces.

5. Cut the ear wire to 1 cm in length. Measure and mark 1 mm from the end of the ear wire, and notch all the way around it with wire cutters at this point. File and sand the tip of the ear wire to round and smooth it. Sand and polish the entire piece.

6. Holding the flattened end of the 16-gauge wire with round-nose pliers, form the wire into a spiral, but don't bend the ear wire.

7. Repeat steps 2 through 6 to make the second earring.

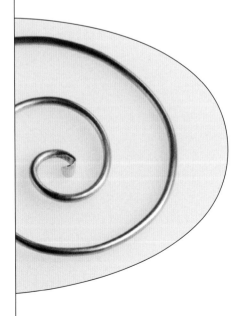

► Get Ready

**SAWING • WIREWORK • SOLDERING • HAMMERING • FILING
SANDING • USING A ROLLING MILL (OPTIONAL) • POLISHING (OPTIONAL)**

►► **Get Set**

Silver wire, 18 gauge

Silver ear wires

Bench tool kit, page 9

Soldering kit, page 9

Bezel mandrel

Ring mandrel

Rolling mill (optional)

Polishing machine
(optional)

FINISHED SIZE
Each hoop, 4.8 x 3 x .01 cm

►►► **Go**

1. Using the jeweler's saw, cut the following lengths of silver wire:

Two pieces, each 10 cm (extra large - **Ⓐ**)

Two pieces, each 7 cm (large - **Ⓑ**)

Two pieces, each 3.5 cm (medium - **Ⓒ**)

2. Using a 6-mm-diameter mandrel, measure and cut two pieces of wire (small - **Ⓓ**), each long enough to form a circle that's 5 mm in diameter. Shape these wires into circles.

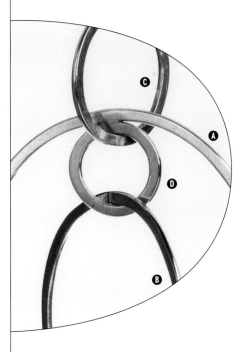

3. Shape the remaining six wires by hand, bending them into more or less round shapes. Solder all the shapes closed. Set the extra large (A) and small (D) shapes aside.

4. Hammer the large shapes (B) on a ring mandrel to create ovals; hammer the medium shapes (C) in the same manner, to create circles. Your hammering will not only shape these wires but will also make them hard and firm after soldering. (To flatten these shapes, you can run them through a rolling mill. If you do, work in incremental stages, gradually taking the wire down to about 0.6 mm in thickness.)

5. Position a small circle (D) against the inner top edge of an extra large oval (A) and solder them together. Repeat with the other two shapes of the same size. Then hammer these parts on a steel block or run them through a rolling mill to flatten them.

6. To assemble an earring, first saw open large oval (B) and a medium circle (C). Then, slip the large oval (B) through the extra small circle (D), and solder the large oval closed. Slip a medium circle (C) through the same extra small circle, and solder it closed. Repeat this process to assemble the other earring in the same manner.

7. Remove any excess solder with a file, and use fine sandpaper to finish all of the parts. For a shiny surface, use a polishing machine or very fine sandpaper. For a matte surface, use a green kitchen scrubbing pad or steel wool. Attach the ear wires to the medium (C) circles.

**USING A DISK CUTTER • DAPPING • CUTTING • FILING
SOLDERING • FINISHING • EPOXY RESIN INLAY**

→► ► **Get Set**

Sterling silver sheet,
   24 gauge, 3.5 x 2 cm

Round sterling silver wire,
   20 gauge, 20 cm

2 tiny jump rings

2 ear nuts

2 diamond-cut sterling
   silver beads,
   approximately 6 mm,
   or other decorative
   elements

Bench tool kit, page 9

Soldering kit, page 9

Disk cutter

Heavy, flathead hammer

Brass bristle wheel

Small bowl of fine rice

Two-part quick drying
   epoxy resin

Toothpicks

Playing card or disposable
   mixing surface

Acrylic color of your choice

Hairdryer

FINISHED SIZE
Each, 1.5 x 1.5 x 1.5 cm

► ► ► **Go**

1. Use a 20-mm disk cutter and a heavy flathead hammer to punch out two 24-gauge sterling silver disks. Dome each silver disk using a dapping block of the appropriate size with a dapping punch and hammer.

2. Cut the 20-gauge silver wire in half to make the ear studs. File a flat surface on one end of each stud. Fit a tiny jump ring snugly around the filed end of each stud. (The jump rings will reinforce the joins between the studs and domes.) Flux and melt a good-sized piece of hard solder onto each wire and jump ring; stop heating the second the solder melts.

3. Place a dome on the soldering block, with its concave surface face down. Flux the center of the dome, and solder the jump-ring end of a stud to it. Repeat this step with the other dome and stud. Pickle, rinse, and dry both pieces.

4. To shine the silver domes, first dip them in soapy water. Then, using the brass bristle wheel in a flex shaft or rotary tool set at a fairly high speed, flick over the surfaces of the wet domes for a few seconds, inside and out.

5. Stiffen both of the annealed studs, by grasping them close to the dome with flat-nose pliers and giving them a firm quarter-twist. Repeat this motion in the middle of the stud and again at its tip. File and sand the ends of the studs to remove any sharp edges.

6. Using the wire cutters and extremely light pressure, grip a stud 4 mm from its end, and twist the earring to cut a notch in the wire. (This groove will help the ear nut click into place and gives a professional look to the finish.) Cut a second groove 2 mm from the end of the wire. The ear nut will click over the end notch to sit between it and the second notch. Repeat with the second stud.

7. To help the epoxy resin form a good bond, score a few small lines in the deepest part of each concave dome with a scribe. Embed the earrings in the small bowl of rice to support the domes while you add the resin.

8. Mix the epoxy resin, following the manufacturer's instructions and blending it with a toothpick. Separate out a third of the resin and mix it with a very small amount of acrylic color. (Caution! Using too much color will prevent the resin from setting properly.)

9. Using the same toothpick, drop some of the colored resin into the bottom of each dome. Carefully place a sterling silver bead in the middle of the resin in each dome. Blast the resin for 30 seconds with a hairdryer set on low heat to speed up the drying.

10. Using a clean toothpick, apply clear resin around each bead, filling the domes to the desired levels. Make sure the clear resin is deep enough to form a bond with the bead. Let the resin cure completely.

34

▶▶ Get Set

Sterling silver sheet,
   24 gauge, 1½ inch
   (3.8 cm) square

Round sterling silver wire,
   20 gauge, 2½ inches
   (6.3 cm) long

Bench tool kit, page 9

Soldering kit, page 9

Photocopied design
   template ❶

Glue

Brass brush

Cup burr

FINISHED SIZE
Each, 3 x 1.7 x 1 cm

▶▶▶ Go

1. Cut out the photocopied design templates and glue them to the sterling silver sheet. Use a jeweler's saw to cut out the two scalloped earring shapes.

2. File around the edges of both silver scallop shapes to create graceful curves.

3. Sand the surface of each silver shape, using circular motions.

4. Use a scribe and ruler to draw lines across the surface of both silver pieces, joining the points where the scallops meet at the edges (as shown on the design template).

5. Place one of the silver pieces on a block of soft wood. Pick up a center punch and a utility hammer. Starting at the points where the scribed lines cross or end, punch small circles along the scribed lines, each about 2 mm apart.

6. Cut two pieces of 20-gauge sterling silver wire, each 3 cm long. File the ends of the wires to square them.

7. Solder one wire to the back of each silver piece, centering it above the intersection of the top pair of punched lines. Pickle the earrings, and then brush them with a brass brush.

8. Using a cup burr attachment on the flexible shaft, round the ends of the ear wires. Use flat and half-round pliers to shape the ear wires.

Have Time to Spare?
These earrings also look great when oxidized.

❶

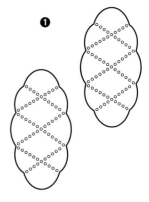

→ Get Ready

ANNEALING • ROLLER PRINTING • USING A DISK CUTTER • FILING
SOLDERING • SANDING • POLISHING • WIREWORK

→▶ Get Set

Sterling sheet, 20 gauge,
    6 x 3 cm

Sterling silver wire,
    12 gauge, 1.5 cm

2 earring posts, 20 or 21
    gauge, with 1.5-mm pad

4 pearl doublets, drilled

2 headpins, 20 gauge, each
    3 inches (7.6 cm) long

2 earring nuts

Bench tool kit, page 9

Soldering kit, page 9

Terry cloth scrap, such as
    a washcloth

Rolling mill

Disk cutter

FINISHED SIZE
Each, 3.5 cm

▶▶ Go

1. Anneal the 20-gauge sterling silver sheet.

2. To texture the dead soft metal, cover one surface with a piece of terry cloth and run this through the rolling mill. If you'd like to texture both surfaces of the metal, sandwich it between layers of terry cloth.

3. Use a disk cutter to cut two matching 1-inch (2.5 cm) circles from the textured metal. (Note: It's often better to cut circles while the metal is work hardened. If you anneal the metal before cutting, the punch has a tendency to bounce, and the circles won't come out as clean.)

4. File the edges of the circles until they're smooth.

5. Using round-nose pliers or a mandrel and the 12-gauge wire, make a jump ring that is 1 cm in diameter. Cut the jump ring in half. File the ends of the half circles smooth and flat.

6. Solder an earring post onto the back of each textured circle, approximately 7 mm from the top edge. Pickle the earrings.

7. Clean the earrings and jump-ring halves. Flux and then solder a half ring to the back of each circle. Position the half ring vertically, directly below the soldered earring posts, and approximately 2 mm from the bottom edge of the circle.

8. Pickle and clean, and then sand and polish the earrings as needed.

9. Feed two pearl doublets onto each headpin. Bend a loop at the top of each head pin, and slip it through the half jump ring on the back of each earring. Wrap the end of the pin around itself three times to secure the pearls.

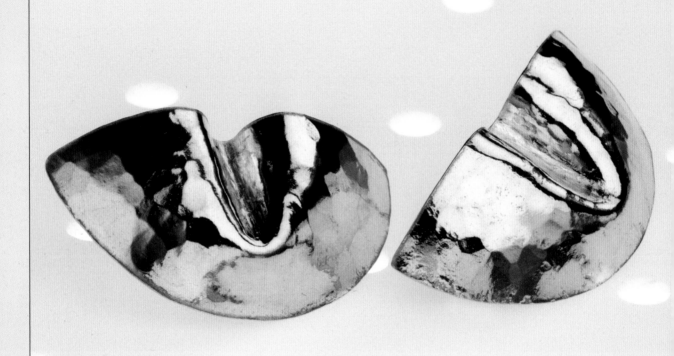

► Get Ready

SAWING • FILING • ANNEALING • DAPPING
PLANISHING • SOLDERING • POLISHING

►► ► Get Set

Silver sheet, 22 gauge,
 4 cm square

2 silver earring posts and
 nuts

Bench tool kit, page 9

Soldering kit, page 9

Small, curved-edge
 planishing hammer

Sandbag

Small creasing hammer

FINISHED SIZE
Each, 3.4 x 1.8 cm

►► ► Go

1. Measure, mark, and cut a 3.5-cm circle from the 22-gauge silver sheet. (Be careful to leave enough silver to cut the two strips called for in step 8.)

2. File the edge of the circle and smooth it with emery paper. Anneal the silver circle.

3. Using a 3-cm depression in a dapping block and the corresponding punch, shape the circle into a dome.

4. With the small, curved-edge planishing hammer, planish the domed circle to give it a hammered texture. Anneal the domed circle.

5. Use a permanent marker to draw a cross on the back of the dome; the lines should intersect at the dome's center.

6. Place the dome face down on a sandbag and, using the small creasing hammer, carefully hammer along one of the marked lines, leaving about 6 mm untouched at each end.

7. Cut the dome in half along the other marked line to produce two earrings. File the rough edges and sand them with emery paper.

8. Cut two 2 x 10-mm strips of silver from your silver waste. Bend the strips so that one side of each is curved to mirror the curve at the top of an earring and the other side is straight.

9. Solder the bent strips to the backs of the earrings, about 5 mm from the top and 3 mm from the straight side.

10. Re-bend the strips as needed to provide a straight platform for attaching the earring posts. Solder the earring posts to the silver strips. Clean and polish the earrings.

➤ Get Ready

**SAWING · SANDING · MELTING WIRE ENDS
DAPPING · DRILLING · WIREWORK**

➤➤ ► Get Set

Sterling silver sheet,
   24 gauge

Round sterling silver wire,
   20 gauge

2 dark-colored rice pearls,
   each 7 mm

2 light-colored beads,
   2 to 6 mm

Bench tool kit, page 9

Soldering kit, page 9

Brass bristle brush

Dapping punch, 1.9 cm in
   diameter

FINISHED SIZE
Each, 5.1 x 1.8 x 1.8 cm

► ► ► **Go**

1. Measure, mark, and cut two sterling silver triangles from the sheet, each with 1¼-inch-long (3.2 cm) sides. Sand the edges of both triangles, and then polish them with the brass brush.

2. Cut two pieces of the 20-gauge sterling silver wire, each 9.5 cm long. Using the torch, melt a ball at one end of each wire. Sand the opposite ends of the wires smooth.

3. Place one silver triangle in a dapping block. Using the 1.9-cm dapping punch and a rawhide mallet, form the triangle so its points face sharply upward. Repeat this process with the second triangle. Give the points of each triangle a firm squeeze with your fingers.

4. Mark the center of each formed triangle with a center punch. Using the flex shaft and 1-mm bit, drill holes at these marks. Also drill holes in the rice pearls or enlarge the existing holes in them.

5. Use sandpaper to remove the burrs left by the drill on the triangles. Give these shapes another quick polish with the brass brush.

6. Onto each piece of balled wire, thread a rice pearl, a light-colored bead, and a formed silver triangle.

7. Using the flat-nosed pliers and the project photo as a guide, make the first bend in each ear wire, approximately 2 cm above the triangle. Make a second bend approximately 1.3 cm away from the first. Gently curve the rest of each wire.

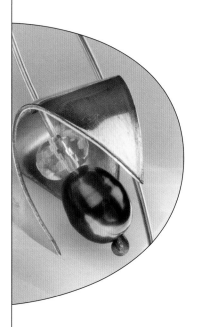

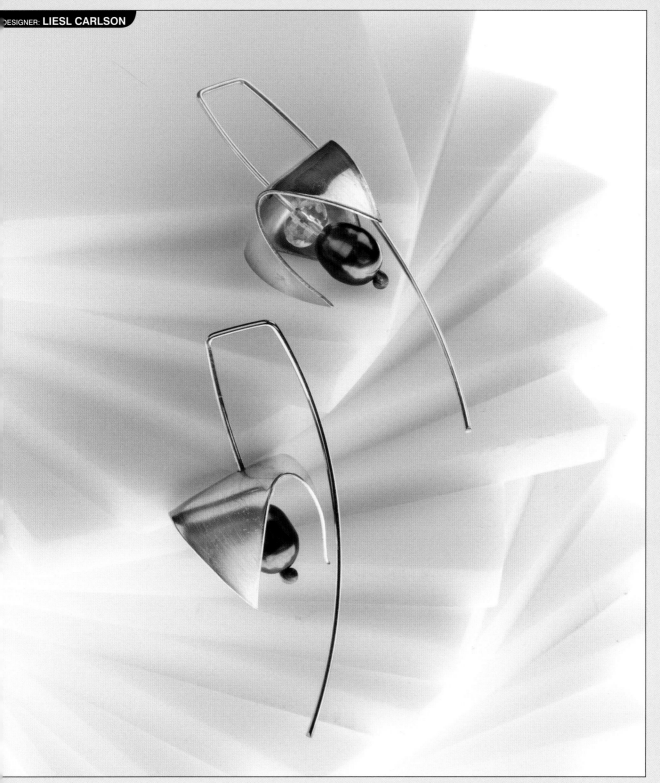

USING A DISK CUTTER • DRILLING • SOLDERING
WIREWORK • FINISHING

→▶ Get Set

Silver sheet, 21 gauge

Silver wire, 30 gauge, 80 cm

2 earring posts, 19 gauge

2 earring nuts to fit the posts

Bench tool kit, page 9

Soldering kit, page 9

Disk cutter and punch

Tumbler or brass brush

FINISHED SIZE
Each, 1 cm in diameter

→▶▶ Go

1. The circular frames for the earrings are made by punching a 4.7-mm hole in a silver sheet, and then punching a 9.5-mm circle around the hole. Start by placing the disk cutter on top of the steel block. Insert the 21-gauge silver sheet into the cutter, and use the hammer and punch to cut out a 4.7-mm hole. Use the mallet to free the punch.

2. Re-insert the silver sheet into the cutter, positioning the small hole you just cut in the center of the 9.5-mm hole in the cutter. Punch a 9.5-mm circle around the smaller hole. Repeat steps 1 and 2 to make the second circular frame.

3. Place the frames on the steel block, and use the mallet to flatten them. Finish them with emery paper.

4. To accommodate the earring posts, drill a hole halfway through the thickness of each earring frame.

5. Use soldering tweezers to insert an earring post into each hole, perpendicular to the earring. Solder the posts in place, using a small amount of flux and a piece of hard solder. Quench and pickle the earrings.

6. Cut the 30-gauge silver wire in half. Starting at the back of an earring frame, close to the earring post, wrap one length of wire in tight circles around the frame. Repeat to wrap the other frame with wire.

7. Using the wire cutters, cut the ends of each wire so that they meet and are flush at the back of each earring. Solder the ends together with a tiny piece of medium solder. Quench and pickle the earrings.

8. In order to create a shiny finish on the wire—one that will contrast beautifully with the whiteness of the silver sheet underneath—place the earrings in a tumbler or use a brass brush to achieve a similar effect.

→► Get Set

14-karat yellow or white
  gold round wire,
  20 gauge, 4 inches
  (10.2 cm) long

14-karat yellow or white
  gold flat wire,
  3.5 mm x 30 gauge,
  4 inches (10.2 cm) long

Bench tool kit, page 9

Soldering kit, page 9

Round bezel mandrel

Soft buffs for flex shaft

Rouge polishing compound

FINISHED SIZE
Each, 3.5 x 1 x 1.2 cm

DESIGNER'S NOTES
You may have to cut the
3.5 mm x 30-gauge strip
from a wider piece of
sheet metal.

To wear these spiral
earrings, twist the round wire
into the pierced earlobe.

►►► Go

1. Cut the 20-gauge round wire in half to make two 2-inch-long (5.1 cm) pieces.

2. Cut the flat wire in half on a diagonal. (The diagonal ends will be at the bottoms of the earrings.)

3. Wrap one flat wire strip around the smallest part of the bezel mandrel, working toward the larger-diameter end and wrapping to the right.

4. Using the round-nose pliers, bend a hook at one end of each round wire.

5. Wrap the round wire around the bezel mandrel, just as you did with the flat strip, in the same direction.

6. Solder the hooked end of the round wire to the flat end of a flat strip.

7. Polish the earring with the soft buff and rouge compound. Wash the earring in hot soapy water and dry it.

8. Repeat steps 3 through 7 to make the second earring, but this time wrap the flat strip and round wire around the mandrel in the opposite direction.

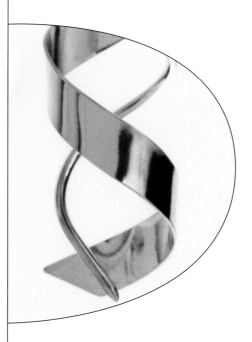

►► Get Set

Sterling silver wire,
    20 gauge, 20 inches
    (50.8 cm) long

Bench tool kit, page 9

Soldering kit, page 9

Wooden dowel, ½-inch
    (1.3 cm) diameter,
    approx. 4 inches
    (10.2 cm) long

FINISHED SIZE
Each, 6.2 x 2 x 1.3 cm

►►► Go

1. Cut the 20-gauge sterling silver wire into two 6-inch-long (15.2 cm) pieces and two 4-inch-long (10.2 cm) pieces.

2. To create an area on each long wire where a short wire can be attached, first measure and mark each long wire, 2 inches (5.1 cm) from one end. Then make marks just above and below the 2-inch (5.1 cm) marks. Using a square metal file, file a flat spot between the outermost marks on each long wire.

3. File one end of each short wire at a slight angle. Fit the angled end of each short wire against the filed spot on each long wire, and check both pairs for a tight fit.

4. Position one set of paired wires on a soldering block so that the filed end of the short wire is snug against the flat spot on the long one.

5. Flux the wires and, heating them slowly, solder them together with easy solder. When the solder has flowed, flip the wires over and ensure a good joint. Quench when finished.

6. Hang the earring by its soldered joint over a free-standing arm. Heat the bottom end of each wire to create a ball of the desired size and shape. Quench, pickle, and clean the soldered wires.

7. Repeat steps 4 through 6 to solder the other two wires together.

8. To create the ear wires, wrap the straight end of each earring around a ½-inch-diameter (1.3 cm) dowel. Using round-nose pliers, create the bends for the branches.

9. Clean and polish the earrings.

DESIGNER: **JANE KROHN**

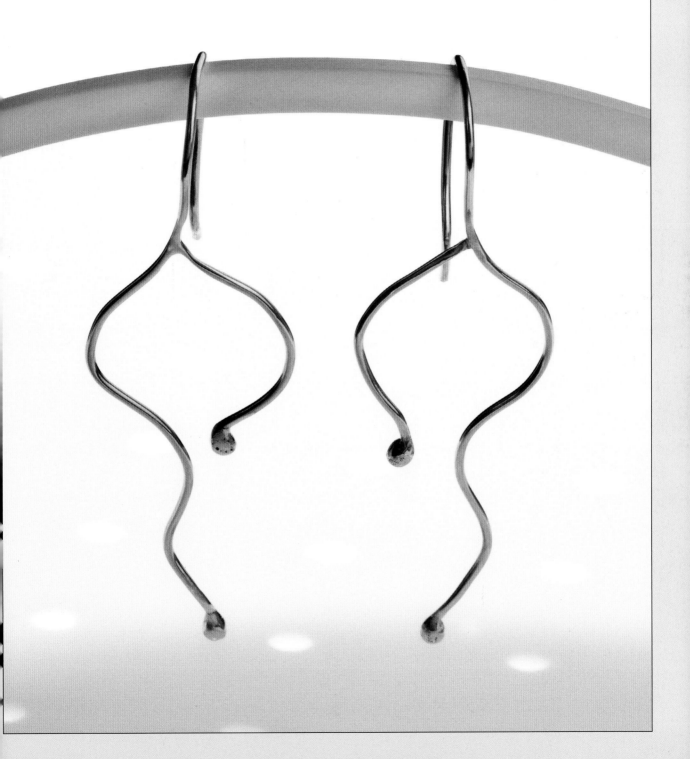

**SAWING • FILING • SANDING • DRILLING • HAMMERING
ANNEALING • SOLDERING • FINISHING • FORMING**

►► Get Set

Round fine silver wire,
    12 gauge, 14 cm

Round sterling silver wire,
    20 gauge, 4 cm

2 earring nuts

Bench tool kit, page 9

Soldering kit, page 9

Ring clamp or vise

Mandrel

FINISHED SIZE
Each, 3 cm in diameter

►►► Go

1. Cut the 12-gauge silver wire into two 7-cm lengths. Measure and mark each piece at 2 cm, 3.5 cm, and 5 cm. File and sand both ends of the cut wires. On one end of each wire, make a divot with the center punch.

2. Clamp one wire in a ring clamp or vise. Drill a 2-mm-deep hole into the end with the divot. Sand off the burrs that formed during drilling.

3. Place the wire on the steel block. Hammer it between the 2 cm and 5 cm marks until the wire is 1 to 2 mm thick. To keep your hammering even, use the 3.5 cm mark as a guide for keeping track of the center.

4. Anneal the wire and quench it in water. Secure the wire in the vise and twist the thinned area.

5. Repeat steps 2 through 4 with the second wire piece, but twist this wire in the opposite direction.

6. To make the ear wires, cut the 20-gauge sterling silver wire in half. Sand and flux both pieces. Fit one ear wire into each hole in the 12-gauge wires, and solder in place. Pickle, rinse, and dry the earrings.

7. Cut each of the ear wires to 1 cm in length. Measure and mark 1 mm from the end of each ear wire. Use your cutters to notch around each ear wire at this point.

8. File and sand the tips of the notched wires to round and smooth them. Sand and polish both earrings and their ear wires. Form the earrings around a mandrel, but leave the ear wires straight.

WIREWORK • SAWING • SOLDERING • FINISHING

▶ Get Set

Flat sterling silver wire,
   0.4 x 1.5 mm,
   80 cm long

Round sterling silver wire,
   16 gauge, 9 cm long

2 sterling silver jump rings,
   18 gauge, each 4 mm OD

2 ear wires

Bench tool kit, page 9

Soldering kit, page 9

Square punch or mandrel,
   6 x 6 mm

FINISHED SIZE
Each, 4 x 1 x 1 cm

▶ ▶ ▶ Go

1. Tightly wrap the flat sterling silver wire around the square mandrel to form it into a coil. Remove the coil from the mandrel, and cut it into two pieces, each 4 cm long.

2. Cut the 16-gauge round silver wire in half.

3. To attach a round wire inside a coil, first bend the two tail ends of the coil inward so that their tips are centered inside the coil. Then insert a round wire into each coil, making sure it's centered in the coil and cradled by the two bent tail ends. Solder the round wires to the bent ends of the coil.

4. Decide which end of the coil to use as the top of the earring, and then solder one jump ring to the end of the round wire.

5. Finish the earrings as desired. Attach an ear wire to each jump ring.

Have Time to Spare?
Here's a unique finishing option that positively glows. Before adding the ear wires, gold plate the earrings then remove the plating from the outer surfaces. The interior of the coil remains plated and remarkably luminous.

VARIATION

→ **Get Ready**

SANDING • SAWING • FILING • SOLDERING • POLISHING

→► **Get Set**

Sterling silver tubing,
  10 mm OD

Sterling silver tubing,
  6 mm OD

Sterling silver tubing,
  1.8 mm OD

2 earring posts and nuts

Bench tool kit, page 9

Soldering kit, page 9

Tube-cutting jig

Buffing wheel

Polishing compound
  of your choice

Tumbler

FINISHED SIZE
Each, 1 x 1 x 0.8 cm

►►► **Go**

1. Sand the ends of each piece of tubing stock to remove scratches. Cut two 3-mm segments from the large-diameter tubing. Cut two 4-mm segments from the medium-diameter tubing. Cut two 10-mm segments from the small-diameter tubing.

2. Square the end of each tubing segment with the file. Clean and degrease the tubing.

3. Place one large-diameter segment of tubing on a firebrick or other soldering surface. With tweezers, insert one small-diameter segment of tubing into a medium-diameter segment, and then place them inside the large-diameter segment. Carefully lift one edge of the large-diameter segment, letting the end of the small-diameter segment drop underneath it. The small-diameter segment should now run diagonally across the inside diameter of the large segment.

4. Apply flux to each of the two areas where the small-diameter tube contacts the large one, and place a solder chip at each junction. (The middle segment will be trapped, but must remain free to wiggle.) Solder the small and large segments together, then pickle the soldered piece.

5. Sand a central portion of the medium-diameter tube and the connecting end of an earring post. Clean and degrease the sanded areas and arrange the earring and post on the firebrick so that the bottom of the post touches the sanded portion of the middle tube. Use a third arm to hold the post in place.

6. Apply flux and a solder chip to the joint. (To prevent the previously soldered joints from detaching, use a solder with a lower melting temperature.) Solder the post in position.

7. Repeat steps 3 through 6 to assemble the second earring. Pickle and rinse the soldered earrings.

8. Polish the earrings on a buff, using your preferred polishing compound. Wash the earrings with dish soap and warm water or in an ultrasonic cleaner. Tumble them to work harden the metal.

DESIGNER: **FEDERICO VIANELLO**

► Get Ready

SAWING • FILING • DRILLING • SOLDERING • WIREWORK

→► **Get Set**

Silver tubing,
   4 mm or larger ID

Silver sheet, 26 gauge

Acrylic rod, 4 mm, color of
   your choice

Sterling silver wire,
   19 gauge

Bench tool kit, page 9

Soldering kit, page 9

Drill bits or round burrs
   in assorted sizes

FINISHED SIZE
Each, 6 x 0.5 x 0.5 cm

→►► **Go**

1. Saw two pieces of silver tubing, each 6 cm in length. File the cut edges smooth.

2. On both tubes, use a scribe to mark locations wherever you'd like there to be holes. Drill holes at the marked locations with a 1-mm drill bit. Enlarge some of the holes by changing to wider bits or to round burrs.

3. Using a round file, smooth the entire inner surface of both tubes.

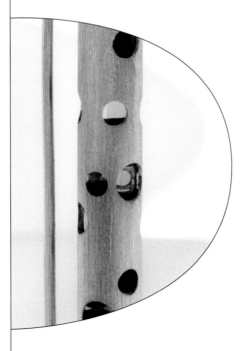

4. To cap the bottom of the earrings, solder a small piece of silver sheet to one end of each tube. Cut off the excess silver sheet with a jeweler's saw. File the silver caps until the edges are smooth and flush with the tubes' exterior surface. Finish with 220-grit sandpaper.

5. Insert the colored acrylic rod into one silver tube. Saw the acrylic flush with the top of the tube. Smooth the cut acrylic edge with 1000-grit sandpaper. Repeat this step for the second tube.

6. To accommodate the ear wires, drill a 1-mm hole through the tube and acrylic rod, 2 mm from the top edge.

7. Cut two 10-cm lengths of silver wire. Use a torch to melt one end of both wires into a little ball.

8. Thread a wire through the hole in one earring. Using a round mandrel and round-nose pliers, bend the wire to form a hook. Trim the wire to match the length of the earring, and sand its ends smooth. Repeat this step for the second earring.

45

→ Get Ready

SAWING • USING A DISK CUTTER • SOLDERING
SANDING • FINISHING

→ ▶ **Get Set**

Sterling silver tubing,
    24 gauge, 6 mm OD

Silver and gold bimetal
    sheet, 0.9 mm,
    1.5 x 1 cm

2 earring posts and nuts

Bench tool kit, page 9

Soldering kit, page 9

Tubing cutter (optional)

Disk cutter

FINISHED SIZE
Each, 1.6 x 0.6 x 0.2 mm

→ ▶ ▶ **Go**

1. Using the tubing cutter or a jeweler's saw, cut four pieces of silver tubing, each 3 mm thick.

2. Cut two disks from the bimetal sheet, each 5 mm in diameter.

3. Arrange two pieces of tubing and one bimetal disk in a vertical row. Solder these elements together, making sure the gold face of the bimetal disk faces forward in the completed earring.

4. Repeat step 3 with the remaining tubing and disk to make the second earring.

5. Solder an earring post to the back of each earring, centering it on the joint between the pieces of tubing.

6. Sand the earrings and finish them as desired.

►► ► Get Set

Sterling silver wire,
   18 gauge, 36 inches
   (91.4 cm)

Sterling silver wire,
   20 gauge, 10 inches
   (25.4 cm)

Bench tool kit, page 9

Soldering kit, page 9

Dowel, 1.8 cm in diameter,
   or dapping tool

Tumbler

FINISHED SIZE
Each, 7 x 1.5 x 1.5 cm

►► ► Go

1. Wrap the 18-gauge wire around the dowel to create a coil of five to six large loops. Using the wire cutters, snip the coil to create jump rings, and file their ends flush. (You'll only need four jump rings, but it's nice to have extras.)

2. Create a sphere from two jump rings by sliding one ring horizontally into another that's positioned vertically. Place the sphere in a third hand and solder the rings together at the points of contact. Pickle the sphere. Repeat this step to make another sphere from two more jump rings.

3. Cut eight pieces of 18-gauge wire, each 1 inch (2.5 cm) long.

4. Make two 90-degree angles in each wire, bending them into the shape of a staple. After bending, each staple shape should be 12 mm long, with two 6-mm-long legs. (The ends of the staple legs must line up with the sphere joints.)

5. Create points on the ends of the staples by cutting two 45-degree angles on each end.

6. Place one sphere on the soldering surface. Using a pair of tweezers, hold a staple against the joints of the sphere, and solder it in place. Repeat to solder three more staples to this sphere. Repeat this step to solder the staples to the second sphere. Pickle the spheres.

7. To create the ear wires, cut two pieces of 20-gauge wire, each 5 inches (12.7 cm) long. File the ends flush. Place a sphere in the third hand and solder one of the ear wires to its top. Repeat with the other sphere. Bend each ear wire to form a hook.

8. Using a file or sandpaper, round out the ends of the ear wires so they'll be comfortable to insert. Place the earrings in the tumbler to finish.

Want to Make Another Pair?

Keen to experiment? This design is well suited for alterations. Change the gauge or shape of the wire, modify the scale of the jump rings—the creative possibilities are limitless!

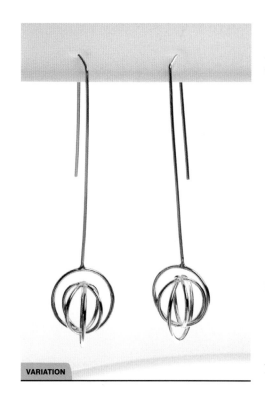

VARIATION

47

→ Get Ready

SAWING · SANDING · FILING · SOLDERING · FINISHING

▶▶ ▶ Get Set

Sterling silver tubing, 2.5 mm OD, 2 mm ID, 8 mm

2 sterling silver earring posts and nuts

Rubber tubing, 2 mm in diameter, 2 pieces, each 5.1 cm

2 sterling silver hollow beads, 8 mm

Plastic connector for rubber tubing

Bench tool kit, page 9

Soldering kit, page 9

Rotary tumbler (optional)

Liver of sulfur or blackening solution (optional)

Wax sealant (optional)

Broken saw blade or straight pin (optional)

Cyanoacrylate glue (optional)

FINISHED SIZE
Each, 1.7 cm in diameter

DESIGNER'S NOTE
Plastic connectors for rubber tubing are sold with the rubber tubing or can be bought separately.

▶▶ ▶ Go

1. Cut the silver tubing in half. Remove any burrs and even the cut edges.

2. With the slim edge of a flat needle file, mark the center point of each silver tube. Flux the marked areas, and solder an earring post to each tube.

3. Finishing options:

• For a shiny finish, polish the sterling silver earring components (the soldered tube and posts and the beads) in rotary tumbler.

• For a blackened finish, place the sterling silver earring components in a warm liver-of-sulfur solution or other blackening agent. Rinse off the blackening solution with water, and dry the pieces completely. Finish all blackened pieces with a wax sealant.

• For a matte finish, buff the sterling silver earring components with a green kitchen scrub or other abrasive material.

4. Push a piece of rubber tubing through each silver tube, centering the tube on the rubber. Slide a silver bead onto each piece of rubber.

5. Insert a 5-mm length of the plastic connector halfway into each piece of rubber tubing. If desired, use a broken saw blade or straight pin to apply a little cyanoacrylate glue to the exposed part of each connector before inserting it into the other end of the rubber tubing to form a circle. Center the beads over the connectors.

VARIATION

48

→ Get Ready

**ROLLER PRINTING • SAWING • FILING • DRILLING
SOLDERING • ADDING A PATINA (OPTIONAL)**

►► Get Set

Silver sheet, 20 gauge,
  1 x 2 inches (2.5 x 5.1 cm)

Small image of a bird,
  traced or photocopied

2 silver ear post and nuts

Silver wire, 18 gauge, 2 cm

2 decorative laminate
  sample chips, any color

Bench tool kit, page 9

Soldering kit, page 9

Heavy textured paper,
  2 sheets

Rolling mill

Cyanoacrylate glue

Glue stick

Masking tape

Liver of sulfur (optional)

Brass brush (optional)

FINISHED SIZE
Each, 4.6 x 1.3 x 0.1 cm

DESIGNER'S NOTES
Find a small, bird silhouette
in a book or on the Internet.
Make sure the bird's feet
join each other or that the
base of the design is solid
enough to hold the
jump ring.

Try your local home-
improvement store or an
architectural firm for sample
laminate chips.

►►► Go

1. Place the 20-gauge silver sheet between two sheets of heavy textured paper. Gently run this stack through the rolling mill. This gives the sheet texture, makes it perfectly flat, and hardens it a bit.

2. Cut the silver sheet in half, and glue the two pieces together with cyanoacrylate glue. Use a glue stick to adhere the traced or photocopied bird silhouette on top of the stacked metal.

3. Carefully saw through the stack to create the two bird forms. To lessen distortion of the bottom bird, keep the saw frame perpendicular to the metal as you cut.

4. File the edges of the bird shapes while they're still glued together. Then separate them, hitting them each with the torch, if necessary, to release the glue.

5. Using a center punch, gently make a small divot on the center back of each bird. Solder an ear post in each divot. Place the birds in the pickle, and while they're in it, make two small jump rings out of the 18-gauge wire.

6. Fasten the laminate sample chips together by wrapping a strip of masking tape around them once. Draw a teardrop shape on the masking tape. Put on a dust mask, and saw through the chips to make two teardrop shapes.

7. Quickly file the edges of the teardrops, and drill a hole at the top of each one to accommodate an 18-gauge jump ring.

8. Remove the birds from the pickle. Harden the ear posts by squeezing them with the flat-head pliers. If needed, drill a hole in the base of the birds to accommodate the jump rings. Using two pairs of pliers, connect each teardrop to a bird with a jump ring.

9. To give these earrings a black patina, dissolve a small chunk of liver of sulfur in a small dish of boiling water. Dip the earrings in this solution; the decorative laminate won't be affected. As the earrings start to darken, brush them often with a brass brush.

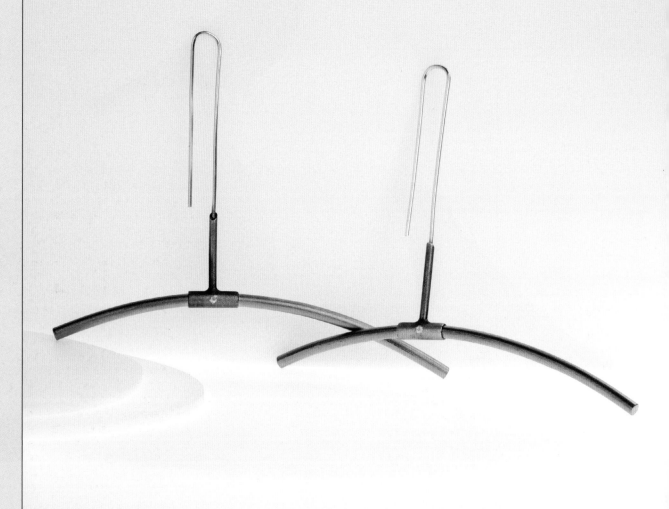

SAWING • FILING • BENDING • SOLDERING • FINISHING
ADDING A PATINA • DRILLING • RIVETING • WIREWORK

► ► **Get Set**

Sterling silver tube,
  2-mm OD, 1-mm ID

Sterling silver tube,
  4.1-mm OD, 3.2-mm ID

Sterling silver wire,
  18 gauge

Round titanium rod or
  aluminum welding rod,
  3.2 mm in diameter

Bench tool kit, page 9

Soldering kit, page 9

Vise

Polishing machine

Matte texturing wheel

White diamond cutting
  compound (optional)

Rouge cloth or buffing
  wheel

Silver oxidizer, such as
  liver of sulfur

Small cross-peen
  rivet hammer

Nail set

Fine jeweler's
  hole-reamer set

Conical burr (setting
  burr or hart burr),
  approximately 5 mm

FINISHED SIZE
Each, 7.6 x 10 x 0.6 cm

► ► ► **Go**

1. Cut two 1.9-cm pieces from the smaller silver tube. File one end of each piece flat and the other at a 45-degree angle. Deburr the filed edges with a fine file. Cut two 1.3-cm pieces from the larger silver tube, file their ends flat, and deburr their edges. Straighten and stretch the silver wire, and cut a 10.8-cm wire piece.

2. Bend the round titanium rod to the desired shape. Cut two 10.2-cm pieces of bent rod. File the ends of these pieces flat, and deburr their cut edges.

3. To create an ear wire, insert a piece of the wire into a small tube until one end of the wire is flush with the flat end of the tube.

4. Make a notch in the soldering brick with the round needle file. Place a large tube in the notch so it won't roll. Place the small tube (with its ear wire) against the center of the large tube to form a 90-degree T joint, with the angle of the small tube pitching downward. Secure the assembly with a third hand or cross-lock tweezers. Flux the assembly, including the top of the small tube, where the wire protrudes.

5. Solder the joint where the two tubes meet with a small chip of medium solder. When the solder has flowed to join the two pieces, add another chip, and "draw" the solder upwards toward the wire. Heat carefully, and stop as soon as you see the solder line at the top of the tube. Pickle, rinse, and dry the piece. Clean up the solder joint, using the round needle file.

6. Firmly insert the end of the ear wire into a vise. Insert a piece of the titanium rod into the larger tube to create a "handle," while maintaining the rod's shape. Pull on the handle very gently to straighten the ear wire. Remove the titanium rod from the tubing.

7. Using a texturing wheel, matte-finish the tubing assembly, taking care not to touch the ear wire. Polish the wire with a rouge cloth or buffing wheel. Touch up the tube with a file, flattening and deburring as necessary. To darken the assembly, dangle it in a container of oxidizer, avoiding the ear wire.

8. Fit the titanium rod into the large tube of the finished assembly. In the featured project, 4.1 cm of rod is exposed at one end.

9. Divot the center of the large tube with a center punch, just below where the narrow tube joins it. Double-check the placement of the titanium rod; then drill a 1-mm hole through the large tube and rod. (Take this critical step slowly, using plenty of beeswax for lubrication. You must bore the hole at exactly 90 degrees.) Deburr the hole.

10. Cut a rivet from the remaining 1-mm wire approximately 6 mm longer than the diameter of the larger tube. Cover the top of the anvil with masking tape so you don't leave marks on the finished earring. Place the earring on the anvil, and insert the rivet wire into the drilled hole by tapping it straight down with the flat part of the hammer. Doing this broadens the rivet to tighten it. Create a rivet head by spreading the end of the rivet with the cross-peen portion of the hammer. Using the nail set, cap the rivet by rotating the tool while gently hammering.

11. Measure and trim the ear wire, 8.9 cm from the end of the small tube. Deburr the wire. Mark the wire 4.4 cm from the top of the tube. Using the pliers, bend a loop, doubling the wire downward. Soften the ear wire to the desired shape with your fingers, and polish it with a rouge cloth.

12. Repeat steps 3 through 11 to create a matching earring.

▶ Get Ready

ROLLER PRINTING • SAWING • SCORING
SOLDERING • BENDING • POLISHING

▶▶ ▶ Get Set

Sterling silver sheet,
  30 gauge, 8 x 6.5 cm

2 sterling silver ear posts
  and nuts

Bench tool kit, page 9

Soldering kit, page 9

Photocopied design
  template ❶

Cardboard

Tulle

Rolling mill

Vise

Wooden craft stick

Polishing cloth

FINISHED SIZE
Each, 6.5 x 2.5 x 1 cm

DESIGNER'S NOTE
If you don't have a rolling
mill, you can buy 32-gauge
sterling silver and texture the
metal sheet by hand with an
engraver.

▶▶ ▶ Go

1. Transfer the photocopied template onto the cardboard, and cut it out.

2. Cover the 30-gauge sterling silver sheet with the tulle. Roll these materials through the rolling mill, reducing the thickness of the sheet to 32 gauge. The tulle-textured surface of the metal will be the front.

3. Using the cardboard template, draw the design twice on the silver sheet. (The narrow, 2-cm end of the design is the top.) Cut out the two drawn shapes. Draw the center dotted line onto the front of the form. Turn the form over and the draw the two dotted lines that are left and right of center on the back.

4. With the metal pieces face up, use a center punch or sharp knife to score along the center line, from the top to the bottom. (Score just deeply enough to make the metal on either side of the line rise upward.) Turn the pieces over, and score along the two side lines.

5. While the pieces are still face down, melt a small amount of silver solder onto the center of each one, 1 cm from the top edge.

6. Using a vise, bend the metal at the carved lines. Flatten the bent lines with the wooden craft stick. (The stick won't damage the metal.) With your hands, bend the sections that are next to the centerline toward the front of the earrings.

7. Solder the ear posts onto the back of the earrings, and polish them.

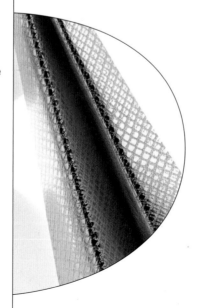

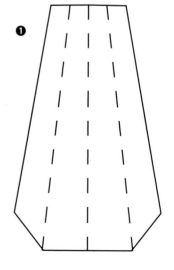

❶

→ ▶ Get Ready

**SAWING • ANNEALING • FOLD FORMING • SOLDERING
ADDING A PATINA • FINISHING**

▶ ▶ Get Set

Copper sheet, 22 gauge,
   3.2 x 4.3 cm

2 earring posts and nuts

Bench tool kit, page 9

Soldering kit, page 9

Photocopied design
   template ❶

Steel pendant wheel

Oxidizing solution

FINISHED SIZE
Each, 4.3 x 0.4 x 1.5 cm

▶ ▶ ▶ Go

1. Using a scribe and ruler, transfer the photocopied design template onto the copper sheet.

2. Cut out the two innermost sections; discard the outer sections. Anneal the two sections that you've kept.

3. Using parallel pliers, fold each copper shape in half along its length, then flatten it with a mallet. Anneal the metal again.

4. To force each shape to curve inward, first place it on a steel block. Working gradually from one end of its longest edge to the other, strike the piece repeatedly with the sharp end of a goldsmith hammer. Turn the shape over and repeat along the same edge on the other side. The shapes should now be gently curved. Focusing on the smaller ends, keep hammering both surfaces until the curve of the metal matches that shown in the project photo.

5. The ends of the earrings should be on the same plane. To even them, scribe and cut a straight line that runs through both ends.

6. Anneal the pieces again. Then pry open the long edges of each one by pushing a scribe between the metal layers and carefully wiggling it. Leave the ends unopened.

7. Using emery paper, clean off a flat area on the small end of each earring. Flux and solder the ear posts to these areas, holding the posts with locking tweezers.

8. Quickly finish the outsides of both pieces with a steel pendant wheel. Brush the oxidizing patina onto the outer surfaces of both pieces, rinse them immediately, and dry them with a cloth.

9. To make the interiors of the earrings shine and to remove any unwanted patina, gently run the steel pendant wheel along the inside surfaces. If desired, rub the thin edges with a burnisher.

❶
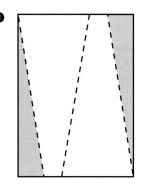

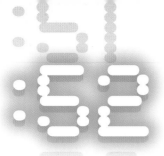

↳ → Get Ready

ROLLER PRINTING • **ANNEALING** • **FILING** • **SANDING**
ANTICLASTIC FORMING • **SOLDERING** • **FINISHING**

→ ► Get Set

Annealed copper sheet,
   24 gauge, 2 x 4 inches
   (5.1 x 10.2 cm)

Annealed sterling silver
   sheet, 24 gauge, plain
   or patterned, 1 x 2
   inches (2.5 x 5.1 cm)

2 round sterling silver
   wires, 20 gauge, each
   2¼ inches (5.7 cm)

Bench tool kit, page 9

Soldering kit, page 9

Manila folder

Hole punch

Rolling mill

Ring pliers or ring mandrel

Dowel, 11 to 12 mm
   in diameter

Anticlastic forming stake

Vise

Nylon forging hammer

FINISHED SIZE
Each, 2.5 x 3.8 cm

DESIGNER'S NOTE

If you don't have a rolling
mill, you can buy patterned
metal, stamp a design, or
go with no pattern at all.

→ ► ► Go

1. Cut a 2 x 4-inch (2.5 x 5.1 cm) piece from the manila folder. Using scissors and a hole punch, create a design in the paper.

2. Sandwich the paper between the copper and sterling silver sheets, and roll them through the mill to transfer the texture. Set aside the patterned copper sheet for another project.

3. Anneal the sterling silver sheet, and then pickle, rinse, and dry it. Measure and cut two ½ x 2-inch (1.3 x 5.1 cm) rectangles from the annealed sheet. File the edges clean and round them slightly. Then sand them with a sanding stick.

4. Using the ring pliers, shape both silver rectangles into circles (they don't have to be perfect), with their textured surfaces facing out. If you don't have ring pliers, use a dowel or a ring mandrel instead

5. Place the forming stake in a vise, and place one silver ring over the groove in the stake. Hammer the ring with the forging hammer to shape it, pinching its ends closed with your fingers as you do (the ring will want to open up as you hammer it). Start along one outer edge (don't hammer right on the edge), and work that whole edge with small, gentle taps, keeping the hammer parallel to the stake, overlapping the taps, and moving the metal, not the hammer, as you progress.

6. Turn the ring around and work the opposite edge. Once you've worked both edges, continue by working towards the middle. (If the ring opens up, remove it from the stake and tap it closed on a wooden block. Put the ring back on the stake and continue forging.) After you've shaped the ring, continue with light hammer strokes to planish the metal smooth. Repeat this step with the other ring.

7. To give the earrings an extra dimension, twist them slightly (in opposite directions) as shown in the project photo, but don't open them up completely.

8. Solder a sterling silver wire to the top surface of the back end of each earring. Pickle, rinse, and dry the earrings.

9. To form the ear hooks, shape each sterling silver wire over a dowel, and then file their ends. Finish the earrings as desired.

Have Time to Spare?

Add a black patina to the textured metal to create more dramatic contrast.

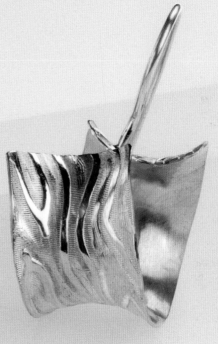

►► ► Get Set

Sterling silver or gold
  sheet, 24 gauge,
  5.5 x 3 cm

2 sterling silver or gold
  wires, 20 gauge, each
  7.6 cm

2 half-drilled Akoya pearls,
  8 mm

Bench tool kit, page 9

Soldering kit, page 9

Disk cutter, 2.5 cm
  in diameter

Goldsmith hammer

Liver of sulfur (if using
  silver)

Burnisher

Epoxy

FINISHED SIZE
Each, 4.5 x 1.5 x 1.5 cm

►► ► Go

1. Using the disk cutter, cut two 1-inch (2.5 cm) circles from the 24-gauge metal sheet. Mark the center of each metal circle.

2. Texture both circles with the goldsmith hammer, starting the lines from the center of each circle and working outward. Also use the hammer to thicken the edges of the circles.

3. With a jeweler's saw, cut a straight 1.3-cm line from the edge of each circle to its center.

4. To shape each metal piece, first use half-round pliers to bend the circle back along its centerline. Then bend up the two corners at the center cut.

5. Solder a 20-gauge wire to the back of the center fold of each earring, leaving 3 mm extending from the bottom of the center cut to hold a pearl.

6. Use half-round pliers to bend the top of each wire into a U shape.

7. Option: If using silver, blacken the earrings with liver of sulfur. Then use a scribe to scribble through the patina on the back of the earring.

8. Finish the earrings by using a medium satin wheel on the outer faces. Burnish the earring edges and back surfaces. Adhere the half-drilled pearls to the ends of the wires with epoxy and let dry.

VARIATION

→ Get Ready

SAWING • SOLDERING • FILING • WIREWORK
HAMMERING • FINISHING

→▶ Get Set

Silver sheet, 24 gauge

Silver wire, 20 gauge

2 silver ear wires

Bench tool kit, page 9

Soldering kit, page 9

2 photocopies of design
   templates ❶

Polishing machine
   (optional)

FINISHED SIZE
Each, 4.5 x 1.5 cm

▶▶▶ Go

1. Transfer the photocopied leaf templates onto the silver sheet. Using a jeweler's saw, cut out the individual leaves.

2. Cut two 2.8-cm lengths, two 4-cm lengths, and two 5.5-cm lengths of the silver wire.

3. Solder a length of wire down the length of each silver leaf: a 2.8-cm wire to each small leaf, a 4-cm wire to each medium leaf, and a 5.5-cm wire to each large leaf. One end of the wire should be at the narrow tip of the leaf and the excess wire should extend past the wider top.

4. Remove any excess solder with a file, and use fine sandpaper to finish all the pieces.

5. Using round-nose pliers, form a small circle at the end of each wire. Bend the wires to create attractive curves, and hammer them on a steel block to harden.

6. For a shiny finish, use a polishing machine or polish the earrings with very fine sandpaper. For matte surfaces, use a green kitchen scrubbing pad or steel wool.

7. With the smallest leaf in front and the largest leaf in the back, slip the wire loops onto the ear wires.

Want to Make Another Pair?
For a two-leaf variation, transfer only the small template onto the silver sheet and cut out four small leaves. Use two 2.8-cm lengths and two 4-cm lengths of silver wire. Solder the wires to different sides of the leaves for each earring,

❶

VARIATION

SAWING • PIERCING • SOLDERING • HAMMERING
ADDING HEAT PATINA • DRILLING • RIVETING

→►► Get Set

Copper sheet, 24 gauge

Silver sheet, 24 gauge

2 earring posts and nuts

Silver wire, 20 gauge

Bench tool kit, page 9

Soldering kit, page 9

2 photocopies of design
    templates ❶

Borax

FINISHED SIZE
Each, 6.2 x 1.7 x 0.1 cm

→►► Go

1. Transfer the photocopied flower templates onto the copper sheet and the stem/leaf templates to the silver sheet. Cut out the four metal pieces with the jeweler's saw.

2. Solder an ear post to the back of each silver stem/leaf, approximately 1.3 cm down from the tip and centered across the width. Make sure to leave enough room in that area to create a rivet nearby (see step 6).

3. Using a hammer and wood block, texture the surfaces of the two silver pieces. Finish these pieces with files and sandpaper.

4. Heat the copper flowers with a torch until they turn red, and then immediately place them in water saturated with borax.

5. Hammer the copper flowers on the steel block, and finish them with the files and sandpaper.

6. Arrange each flower on top of a stem/leaf, and using the project photo as a guide, drill a 0.8-mm hole through each paired set. Rivet the parts together with the 20-gauge silver wire.

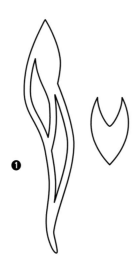

❶

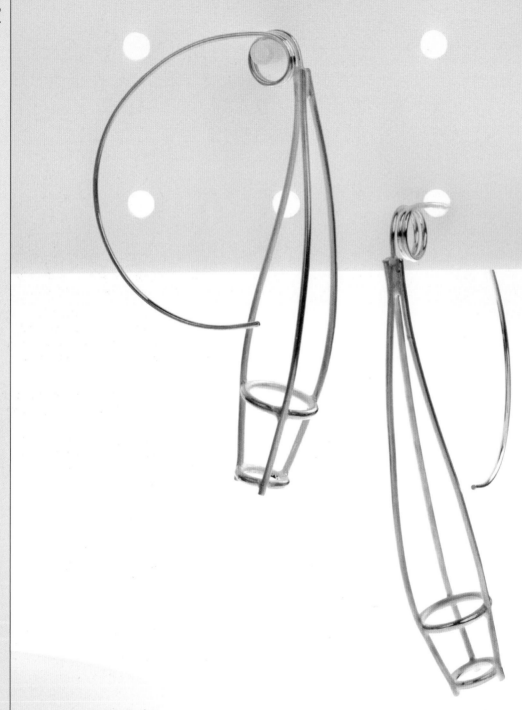

WIREWORK · SAWING · SOLDERING · FILING
FINISHING · RAISING FINE SILVER

►► ► Get Set

2 sterling silver wires,
   18 gauge, each 15.2 cm

6 sterling silver wires,
   16 gauge, each 8.3 cm

Sterling silver wire,
   14 gauge

Bench tool kit, page 9

Soldering kit, page 9

Vise

2 mandrels or drill bits,
   0.6 cm and 1 cm

Soft brass bristle hand
   brush

Burnisher

Optional finishing supplies:
   polishing lathe, matte
   texturing brush for
   lathe, polishing buff,
   white diamond cutting
   compound

FINISHED SIZE
Each, 8.9 x 3.8 x 0.6 cm

►►► Go

1. Secure one end of the 14-gauge silver wire to the 0.6 cm mandrel by clamping them in the vise. Twist the wire around the mandrel, creating a coil with at least two loops.

2. With the jeweler's saw, cut perpendicular to the spiral's core to separate each of the two loops from the coil. Using parallel-jaw pliers, bend the cut ends of each loop to form a ring. Solder each ring closed with hard solder. Pickle and clean each ring.

3. At the joint of each ring, use the round needle file to make a notch on the exterior. Using dividers and the filed notches as starting points, divide each ring into three equal parts. File two more notches on each ring at the marked points.

4. Repeat steps 1 through 3 to make two more notched rings, this time using the 1-cm mandrel.

5. Place a smaller notched ring on the soft soldering brick. Push three 16-gauge wires into the brick, about ⅛-inch (0.3 cm) deep, locating one wire at each notch. Solder the wires to the ring with medium solder. Pickle the ring, and clean up any solder debris.

6. Using your fingers, gently spread the three wires to create the desired shape. Place the assembly back into the holes in the soldering brick. Fit one of the larger rings inside the three wires, trapping it about ½ inch (1.3 cm) above the first ring. Solder the larger ring to the wires with medium solder, being careful not to re-melt the joints in the smaller ring. Pickle and clean the piece.

7. Bend the wires by hand to create a graceful flow of lines that converge at one end. Trim all wire ends with the jeweler's saw, file them flat, and deburr them. Using pliers, gently bend the wire ends to create a ⅛-inch-long (0.3 cm) parallel union at the top.

8. Insert one of the 18-gauge wire lengths into the center of the three coverging wires. Double check that the wires are parallel and fit together well. Solder this joint with easy solder. Pickle, rinse, and dry this piece.

9. Remove any solder debris from the earring with a needle file. If desired, create a matte finish on the earring (but not on the ear wire) with a texturing brush, polishing buff, and white diamond compound.

10. On a clean soldering brick, gently warm the earring until it turns black, taking care to avoid the ear wire and not to melt the easy solder. Let the earring cool, pickle it, rinse it, and brush it with the brass brush to burnish the fine silver on the surface. Repeat this step three times, but the third time, don't use the brass brush.

11. Use a burnisher to highlight the outer edges of the earring wires. Pull the burnisher along the ear wire several times as you support the wire with the forefinger of the same hand; the pressure applied will form a natural curve in the wire. File the ear wire end, removing the burr.

12. To create the loop in the ear wire, wrap it around the ¼-inch (0.6 cm) mandrel, being careful not to snap the sensitive joint where the four wires meet. Shape the ear wire as desired.

13. Repeat steps 6 through 12 to make the matching earring. Note: the two earrings don't have to be symmetrical.

►► Get Set

Silver clay (PMC3),
   8 to 10 grams

Thick silver clay paste
   (PMC3), stirred well

2 silver wires, 20 gauge,
   each 1.6 cm

2 fine silver earring posts
   and nuts

Half-drilled freshwater
   pearls, 8 mm white (2)
   and 6 mm pink (2)

Bench tool kit, page 9

Kiln with kiln shelf

Mug warmer

Dehydrator

Lubricant, non-petroleum-
   based balm or olive oil

Palette plate

2 shallow-textured rubber
   stamps on wood blocks

Deck of playing cards or
   rolling slats in different
   thicknesses

Clear acrylic sheet or
   disassembled CD
   jewelcase

Humidifier or other means
   of preserving moisture

2 nonstick, heat-resistant
   surfaces, 10.2 cm
   square and 5.1 cm
   square

Fine-pointed paste brush

Crumb brush

Stainless steel pan

Kiln tongs

Liver of sulfur

3 radial bristle disks

Aluminum oxide cylinder
   point for refining, 330 or
   similar grit

Quick-drying gel epoxy

FINISHED SIZE
Each, 3 x 0.8 x 1.5 cm

DESIGNER'S NOTE
To complete this project in
30 minutes, read through the
instructions and set up the
tools required for each step.

►►► Go

1. Remove the kiln shelf from the kiln. Set the kiln to full ramp, 1650°F (899°C) and hold for 20 minutes. Turn on the mug warmer and dehydrator. Apply a light coat of lubricant to both rubber stamps. Place the palette plate face down on your work surface. Measure and mark a point that is 8 cm up the side of the dome. Measure and mark this point on a second dome.

2. Open your package of metal clay, cut off what you need, and place the rest in the humidifier. Place two sets of 16 cards each or rolling slats of equivalent thickness on your work surface, about 3 inches (7.6 cm) apart. Place the measured metal clay between the two stacks, and use a roller to roll back and forth over the clay until it no longer stretches.

3. Cut a 10.2-cm piece from the rolled clay. Then cut that length in half. Cut a 1.3-cm piece from the outer end of each 5.1-cm piece. You now have two long and two short pieces. Place these pieces in the humidifier.

4. Set one oiled rubber stamp on your work surface, rubber side up. Place two sets of eight cards each on the stamp, about 2.5 cm apart. Position one of the long clay pieces vertically between them. To create a pattern on the clay, roll back and forth over the clay with the second stamp until it is flush with the cards. Remove two cards from each stack, and press the clay into the base stamp with the upper stamp block.

▶ ▶ ▶ Continued

5. Drape the clay over a dome on the underside of the palette plate, allowing one end to bend to the mark you made at 8 cm. (You'll place your ear post at this bend later.) Place the palette plate into the running dehydrator. Repeat step 4 with the second long strip, returning the palette plate to the dehydrator after adding a new strip.

6. Using a six-card thickness, roll each of the shorter pieces as you did in step 4. Then remove two cards and press the clay into the lower stamp with the roller so one side is smooth. Drape the strips over your palette plate domes with their smooth sides down, and return the plate to the dehydrator.

7. Leave the palette plate in the dehydrator for two minutes to allow the clay strips to set. Then, to allow for more air circulation, remove them from the plate, and place them in the dehydrator on their edges for two more minutes. Remove the strips from the dehydrator, and return the long strips to the domes.

8. On each long strip, make a dimple two-thirds of the way down from the bend. Make a dimple in the center of the textured side of each short strip. Place a tiny drop of water on each dimple. After a few seconds, place a small dollop of metal clay paste on each dimple. Wait a couple of seconds, then connect each small strip to a large one at the dimples, and wiggle them together just a little. Hold in place and count to 20.

9. Place the earrings on the hot mug warmer for one minute, with their large arches facing up. With tweezers, turn them over onto their edges and wait another minute. Remove them with tweezers and place them on a cold stainless steel pan to draw out the heat. After a few seconds, test them carefully; the first piece should be cool enough to touch.

10. Mark and lightly scratch each earring in the curve of each small arch. Drill a slightly angled hole at each mark, through the entire earring. Check that the small pieces of silver wire fit through the holes.

11. Place the earrings on their sides on a nonstick surface. Trim any unevenness and clean up any rough edges with the fine emery board. Using the coarse emery board, lightly add vertical texture to the smooth side of each small arch, and lightly texture any edges to blend with the texture on the earrings. Brush well with the crumb brush.

12. Flip the earrings over and balance them on their small arches. Place a small drop of water on the bend at one end of each, and wait a few seconds. Apply a small dab of paste clay to the damp area, and position an earring post in the paste, moving it around slightly to set it.

13. Balance the earrings on the hot mug warmer, on their small arches, for one minute. Then flip them over with tweezers and let them heat for another minute. Set the earrings on the cold stainless steel pan for a few seconds.

14. Slide the silver wires into the drilled holes, centering each one in its earring, and place the earrings on a kiln shelf, on their sides. Using long tongs, quickly place the shelf into the hot kiln, and close the door. Fire for 10 minutes. While the earrings are being fired, mix a liver of sulfur solution. With long tweezers or tongs, remove the earrings from the kiln and quench them. Use the radial bristle disk to bring up the silver quickly.

15. Dip the earrings into the liver of sulfur solution a couple of times, then rinse them. Use the radial bristle disk to bring up the raised areas, then switch to the cylinder point to remove the patina from the front of the small arch and add a little more scratchy texture.

16. Straighten the wires so they're perpendicular to the earrings, and carefully trim them to length. Place a drop of quick-dry gel epoxy into each half-drilled pearl hole, and fit the small pearls onto the small-arch wires, and the large pearls onto the large-arch wires. Wick away any excess glue with the corner of a paper towel.

MELTING METAL • **SOLDERING** • **SAWING** • **FILING**
DRILLING • **POLISHING** • **BEZEL SETTING**

►► ► Get Set

Sterling silver or clean
sterling silver scrap,
approximately 5 dwts

2 square sterling silver
wires, 14 gauge,
each 6.4 cm

2 sterling silver tube
bezels with precut seats
for 3.5-mm stones

2 round faceted blue topaz,
each 3.5 mm

2 round hard sterling silver
wires, 20 gauge,
each 7.6 cm

Bench tool kit, page 9

Soldering kit, page 9

Disk-cutting punch, 2.2 or
2.5 cm in diameter or
small, polished steel
block

Steel ring mandrel

Small ball burr

Tripoli and rouge polishing
compound

Liver of sulfur

Bezel pusher

FINISHED SIZE
Each, 2.5 x 2.2 x 0.4 cm

►► ► Go

1. To make the textured element for the center of the earring, place 2.5 dwts of silver or silver scrap in the middle of a charcoal block. Heat the metal with a torch until it forms a molten circle that appears to vibrate. Hold the disk-cutting punch or the steel block in one hand, very close to the melted metal. Remove the torch flame and immediately flatten the molten metal with the punch or block. (If you slam down the punch too hard, the resulting silver piece will be paper thin, but if the punch comes down too slowly, it will barely flatten the silver.) The element should be 1.9 to 2.2 cm in diameter and irregular in shape.

2. Repeat step 1 to make a second silver element. Pickle and rinse both elements. One surface of each will have more texture than the other surface.

3. Using half-round pliers, shape each piece of square silver wire into a circle. Use a saw or file on the ends to achieve a flush fit. Solder each circle closed with hard silver solder. Place one circle on a ring mandrel and tap it with a rawhide hammer to form a perfect circle. Repeat with the second circle. Then tap both circles flat on a polished steel block.

4. Place one soldered circle on top of one textured silver element, making sure the solder joint of the circle is at 12 o'clock. Arrange these pieces so half of the textured piece rests inside the bottom half of the circle and half of the textured piece is outside it. Rotate the textured element until the section that's inside the frame appeals to you. Using a marker, draw the inside curve of the frame onto the textured element.

5. Using a jeweler's saw, cut along the marked line on the textured element. With a large flat file, refine the curve of the cut so it makes continuous contact with the inside curve of the frame. Solder the frame and disk together, using hard or medium solder.

6. Repeat steps 4 and 5 to cut second element and solder it to the remaining circle.

7. Position a tube bezel on each silver circle so it covers the original solder joint; the top of the bezel should sit above the circle. Solder the bezels in place with a small amount of medium solder.

8. For the ear wire holes, mark a centered point on each bezel at the 12 o'clock position and a little more than half way down the tube. Divot each mark with a small ball burr. Drill a hole on each bezel at the divot.

9. Polish the circles with Tripoli compound. Polish the textured elements only if they have sharp areas that require smoothing. Place the earrings in hot liver of sulfur solution for 30 seconds. Remove them and rinse with hot water.

10. Set a topaz in each bezel, using the bezel pusher. To support the bezel during this step, insert a piece of 1.5 mm square wire or sheet underneath the bezel's overhanging portion. Buff the bezel and circle with tripoli and rouge compounds. Lightly buff the oxidized texture with rouge compound if desired.

11. Using round-nose pliers, turn a 1.9-cm open circle at one end of each piece of 20-gauge round wire. Form each wire into a U shape by bending it in the middle. Slip the open end of the circle through the hole in the tube bezel, then squeeze it closed with the chain-nose pliers. Lightly curve the other end of each ear wire with half-round pliers.

► Get Ready

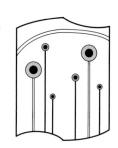

❶

► ► Get Set

Polystyrene plastic sheet,
14 gauge

Cuttlefish-bone section,
6.4 x 7.6 cm

22-karat yellow gold round
wire, 22 gauge

Sterling silver casting grain,
14 grams

Sterling silver tubing,
6.5 mm OD

2 sterling silver round
wires, 20 gauge, 5.1 cm

Bench tool kit, page 9

Soldering kit, page 9

Photocopied template ❶

2 charcoal blocks

Carving tools

Oil-based modeling clay

Crucible

Round burrs, 1.9 and 2.9 mm

Radial bristle discs, 400 grit

Extra-fine polishing pin

Casting flux

FINISHED SIZE
Each, 3.2 x 1.2 x 0.2 cm

DESIGNER'S NOTE

Prepare a casting station in
advance that is completely
level and fire-resistant.
Ensure that the larger
charcoal block is completely
flat and position kiln bricks
around it to shield you from
splatters of molten metal.

► ► ► Go

1. Transfer the photocopied template onto
the polystyrene sheet, using a circle template
to draw the arcs. Cut out the polystyrene
template with heavy shears.

2. To prepare the mold, place a piece of
sandpaper on a hard surface and sand the
soft interior of the cuttlefish bone. Brush the
cuttlefish off to clean it.

3. To make the gold flowers, wrap the gold
wire two-and-a-half times around needle-
nose pliers. Cut the coiled wire in half, and
hammer each wire to flatten it to the desired
shape.

4. To make the granules, snip varying
lengths of gold wire (2 to 5 mm long),
and place them at one end of the smaller
charcoal block. Hold the block at an angle, a
foot (30.5 cm) above a pan of water. Melt the
snipped wire pieces with a torch until they
draw into spheres, then allow them to roll off
the block into the water.

5. Press the plastic template into the soft
face of the cuttlefish bone, remove it, and
brush the bone clean. Repeat two to three
times until the cavity in the bone is as thick
as the template.

6. Carve the desired line work into the mold
(for example, stems and curves). To create
straight lines quickly, press a sharp cutting
tool into the surface; curved lines can be
carved with a pencil. Brush the surface clean.
Use a sharp tool to carve vents around the
perimeter of the mold.

7. Press the gold flowers and granules
into the mold. Ensure that they're properly
positioned, or they may come loose during
casting.

8. Attach the modeling clay firmly to the
back of the bone, over the earring cavity, and
shape it into a handle that will give you a firm,
level grip.

9. Melt the sterling silver casting grain in
the crucible, and then carefully pour it on
top of the charcoal block. Reduce the flame
and continue heating the metal from directly
above until it's completely molten. A perfectly
level block should hold the molten metal in
its center.

10. While removing the flame, press the
mold on top of the molten metal, holding the
mold by its clay handle and using firm, even
pressure. Quickly and carefully, remove the
mold from the block and quench.

11. Using a 4/0 saw blade, remove the
excess metal from around the perimeter of
the casting. Finish the edges with a half-
round file. Split the cast sheet in half by
sawing along the vertical centerline.

12. Using round burrs, cut different sizes of
flower cups in the cast metal pieces. With a
2/0 saw blade, cut vertical stems to the base
of each burred cup. Drill holes in the centers
of the flowers.

13. Cut two 1.5-mm sections of silver
tubing. Solder one on the back of each
earring, centered across its width. Pickle the
earrings.

14. Form two ear wires from the 20-gauge
wire, and suspend the earrings from the
loops. Lightly polish the gold and raised
textures on each earring with the radial bristle
disk. Polish and brighten the insides of the
drilled flower cups with a polishing pin.

► ► Get Set

22-karat bimetal, 24 gauge, 1.6 cm square

Ginbari fine silver foil

Half-hard brass, 18 or 20 gauge, 5.1 cm square

2 earring posts, 20 gauge

2 round silver wires, 20 gauge, each 1.3 cm

2 half-drilled white pearls, each 5 mm

Bench tool kit, page 9

Soldering kit, page 9

Abrasive cleanser

Soft toothbrush

Tracing paper

Stencil, 1.6 cm square

Copper, brass, or steel sheet, 10.2 x 10.2 x 0.6 cm

Hotplate

Fine tweezers

Fine-tipped paintbrush

Kiln gloves

2 curved burnishers

Rice paper, 1½ inches (3.8 cm) square

Rolling mill

Bench vise

Forming block and wooden dowel, ¼-inch (0.6 cm) diameter

Soft brass bristle brush

Liver of sulfur

Ammonia

Wax sealant (optional)

Soft cloth

Two-part epoxy

FINISHED SIZE
Each, 2.2 x 0.6 x 0.2 cm

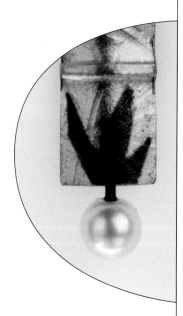

► ► ► Go

1. Clean the bimetal square with abrasive cleanser and a wet, soft toothbrush. Flux and anneal the bimetal with the gold side down. Let it cool, then quench and pickle it.

2. Place the silver foil inside a folded a piece of tracing paper, at its crease. Draw two similar three-leaf designs—each approximately 0.6 cm square—on the paper. Cut out the foil leaf shapes.

3. Measure and mark a centerline on the gold surface of the bimetal square. Place the square on the 10.2-cm metal sheet, and set the sheet on top of the hotplate. Using tweezers, arrange the foil leaf shapes along the bottom edge of the bimetal, one on each side of the centerline and at equal distances from it. Adhere the foil to the gold by applying water with the fine-tipped paintbrush.

4. Turn on the hotplate, setting it at medium. The time it takes to fuse the metals is usually around 3 minutes and 15 seconds. Put on kiln gloves, and pick up a burnisher in each hand. To test each foil shape for adherence, use the pointed end of one burnisher to hold down the bimetal while pressing the center of the foil with the other burnisher's curved surface. When the foil begins to adhere, use the curved burnisher to continue pressing the foil to the metal square, working from the foil's center toward its edges. Using tweezers, place the fused piece on the steel block to air cool.

▶ ▶ ▶ Continued

5. Place the rice paper fiber side down on the half-hard metal sheet. Then place the gold surface of the bimetal face down on top. Roll the sandwiched pieces through the mill, with the fused-leaf surface at the bottom so that it enters the rollers last. Use just enough pressure to emboss the metal. Flux and anneal the bimetal piece, gold side down. Air cool it, and then pickle.

6. Set the bimetal piece in a small vise, with the fused foil at the bottom and the gold side facing you. Close the vise about 3 mm above the top of the foil leaf so 6 mm of gold remains above the jaws. With the rawhide mallet, hammer the gold surface away from you to form a right angle. Remove the piece from the vise, place it on the steel block, and finish folding it in half with the mallet, flattening the edge of the fold as you do.

7. Flux and anneal the piece, foil side down (facing away from the flame), then air cool and pickle it. Dry it thoroughly, then pry it open with the utility knife. If necessary, pickle and dry it again. To open the piece completely, first place it on the steel block, with the fold on the edge of the block, and strike the gold side with the mallet. Then place the piece on the flat surface of the block, and continue to strike it.

8. Pass the piece through the rolling mill, without pressure, and with its fold line at a right angle to the rollers. Gently add pressure until a flat top appears on the fold line. This should take two easy passes.

9. Place the piece in a 1.6-cm square stencil. Using the steel ruler and scribe, trace a square on the gold surface, and a centerline that separates the two leaf shapes. Saw the piece apart along the centerline. File both pieces into matching rectangles and remove all burrs.

10. Place one of the rectangles, gold side down, in a curve in the forming block. Center a 0.6-cm wooden dowel along its length and strike the dowel with the mallet to form a soft curve in the rectangle. Repeat with the other rectangle.

11. Solder an earring post just above the fold line of each earring, using medium solder. Air cool and pickle both pieces.

12. To add a peg for the pearl, first protect the earring post by attaching self-locking tweezers to its base. Place one piece of the 20-gauge silver wire in a second pair of self-locking tweezers, and solder the wire to the center bottom of the rectangle (under the leaf shape) with easy solder. Air cool the earring and pickle it. Repeat this step to add a peg to the other earring.

13. Brush the earrings with a soft bristle brass brush and soapy water, handling them by their edges to keep them free of grease. Make a liver-of-sulfur solution and patinate the earrings until the silver turns dark gray. Rinse the earrings in cold water and dry them. Apply the wax according to the manufacturer's instructions, avoiding the pearl peg as you do.

14. Using flush cutters, trim the peg lengths to fit through the pearls, leaving just a bit of wire to show below each pearl. Mix the two-part epoxy and glue the pearls onto the pegs. Stand the earrings with the pearls at the top and allow the epoxy to dry.

CONTRIBUTING DESIGNERS

Eleni Avloniti is a jewelry designer from the small Greek island of Corfu. She strives to create art that shows the marriage between simplicity and form. Most of her inspiration for jewelry comes from traveling and from her Mediterranean surroundings. For further information, visit www.mod3rnart.com.

Boris Bally's award-winning work is both witty and innovative. His current repertoire transforms recycled street signs, weapon parts, and other found materials into objects for the home and body. Boris has received several prestigious fellowships, and his work is featured in numerous international exhibitions and publications.

Raïssa Bump teaches and makes jewelry and knitwear. She is thrilled to contribute her own designs to the rich history of adornment. More of her work can be seen at: www.raissabump.com.

Lisa Cain is an artist, educator, punster, and glamorous grandmother. She has been making jewelry for 18 years and is executive director of The Mid Cornwall School of Jewelry in England. She also runs the PMC Guild U.K., is fascinated with the Tudors, and loves to drive her Mini Cooper.

Liesl Carlson resides in Layton, New Jersey, where she maintains a studio creating one-of-a-kind work and limited edition pieces. E-mail her at: lcarlsonjewelry@gmail.com.

Charles Carubia started making jewelry in the 1970s while studying at the School of Visual Arts in New York. He is a member of the Florida Society of Goldsmiths and the Saint Augustine Art Association. Charles specializes in custom design and makes one-of-a-kind pieces that incorporate 30 years of knowledge. Contact him at: carubias@bellsouth.net.

Marea Chernoff began metalsmithing in 2002 as a hobby and instantly discovered a passion for designing and creating metal jewelry. Her teacher and inspiration over the years has been jeweler Dominique Bréchault. In 2008, Marea turned hobby into business and created Marea Studio Designs, selling locally in Vancouver and online at www.mareastudiodesigns.com.

Thea Clark first made jewelry in 1991 and began teaching in 1999. She loves to combine materials and techniques, aiming for innovation and unique design along the way. She can't imagine life without her rolling mill. Visit www.theaclark.com, or contact the artist at theaclark@verizon.net.

Vicki Cook lives and hammers in southwest Michigan, where she is a proud member of Chartreuse Co-op Art Gallery. Her website is www.vcmetalworks.com, and her adventures in hammering are documented at vicki-cook.blogspot.com. Vickie's little studio full of hammers can be found at 210 Water Street, Benton Harbor, Michigan, 49022.

Ross Coppelman has been hand-fabricating jewelry on Cape Cod for nearly 40 years. Primarily self-taught, he first learned the blobbing technique from Bernard Kelly in the early '70s, but hasn't used it until now. Ross maintains a year-round showroom and workshop in East Dennis, Massachusetts. Find him online at: www.coppelman.com.

Heather Crossley is an experimental mixed media artist who delights in turning discarded objects into artful and purposeful things. Originally from Singapore, Heather now resides in Brisbane, Australia. She can be contacted at mkhc@powerup.com.au. More of her work can be seen at homepage.powerup.com.au/~mkhc.

Dilyana Evtimova lives and works in West Midlands, United Kingdom. She is trained in multiple disciplines and has a degree in 3-D contemporary applied arts from University of Wolverhampton. Dilyana produces jewelry for retail and private commissions and tries to capture the fragility of organic forms in her work. E-mail: hdilyanadesigns@hotmail.co.uk.

Deborah Fehrenbach is a working artist and teaches at her local art center. She can be contacted at: deborahmarie@mutualdata.com.

Elizabeth Glass Geltman and Rachel Geltman are a mother and daughter jewelry design team in Washington, D.C. Their creations have been published in numerous books, magazines, and newspapers. Visit them at www.geltdesigns.com.

Ellen Gerritse loves to explore and experiment with materials and techniques. As a free thinker (the result of extensive traveling), she creates unusual pieces. Her device: think beyond boundaries.

Joanna Gollberg is a studio jeweler in Asheville, North Carolina. She exhibits and sells her jewelry nationally and teaches jewelry making for metalsmithing groups and craft schools. Joanna is the author of four Lark Books' publications: *Making Metal Jewelry, Creative Metal Crafts, The Art and Craft of Making Jewelry,* and *The Ultimate Jeweler's Guide.*

Amanda Shero Granström is a fiber and jewelry artist splitting her time between Buffalo, New York, and Portland, Oregon. She enjoys designing and making wire and chainmaille jewelry and offers instruction, kits, and supplies on her website at www.redeftshibori.com. E-mail her at: amanda@redeftshibori.com.

Alison Hanlon is a silversmith and jeweler specializing in innovative sculptural bowls and jewelry. She primarily uses a creasing technique, which allows the malleability of metal to determine designs. The coastline of Cornwall, England, inspires her work, which can be viewed at www.alisonhanlon.co.uk. Contact her at alisonhanlon@yahoo.co.uk.

Rebecca Hannon graduated from Rhode Island School of Design and worked as a goldsmith in New York City before attending the Akademie der Bildenden Kuenste in Germany on a Fulbright scholarship. She now teaches, lectures, and has a workshop in Ithaca, New York. Her work can be found internationally in public and private collections.

Kim Harrell is a Colorado native but lived and worked in London, England, for 14 years. She designed contemporary silverware and jewelry for galleries, department stores, and museums. Kim returned to Colorado to establish a studio and gallery, East End Applied Arts. She develops collections for wholesale, retail, and private clients.

Ellen Himic has designed jewelry for more than a decade. Her artwork can be seen in galleries worldwide and has been published in numerous books. Ellen graduated with various awards from Tyler School of Art, esteemed for its world-renowned professors and emerging technologies.

Dorothea Hosom is a studio metalsmith with a particular interest in enamel and mixed media jewelry. Her work is included in Lark Books' *500 Earrings, 500 Brooches, 500 Enameled Objects,* and *The Art of Jewelry: Paper Jewelry.*

Laura Itkonen is a designer from Finland who preserves memories by converting old videotape and cassette tapes into jewelry. E-mail her at: laura_itkonen@hotmail.com.

Taya and Silvija Koschnick grew up working in their mother's bead store where they came to appreciate designing with rare and unusual beads. They formed Tasi Designs jewelry (www.tasidesigns.com) in Portland, Oregon. Tasi Designs blends new, antique, and ancient components to create unique jewelry with a modern aesthetic.

Jane Krohn is a metal artist from Seattle, Washington. She has been melting, soldering, and creating with metals and other organic elements for over 20 years. She loves all things simple and quirky and can be found at www.janekrohn.com.

Melissa Lew is an award-winning artist whose sculptural jewelry is influenced by her Chinese heritage, especially the culture's deep respect for nature. She earned a BA in art and visual technology from George Mason University, and her work and has been exhibited throughout Washington, D.C. Visit www.melissalew.com or contact melissa@melissalew.com.

Donna Lewis is a metal clay artist and educator whose work is included in several publications. As a Wisconsin native, her creativity developed while avoiding the bitter cold and those gigantic mosquitoes. Now in warm, sunny Arizona, she shares her artistic nature with students and spends her favorite time feeding the metal clay addiction.

Ann L. Lumsden is a goldsmith, designer, and Ottawa native. She strives to create pieces that are contemporary and classic. Through ongoing explorations of materials and techniques, both traditional and avant-garde, her work continues to evolve. She is a member of the Metal Arts Guild of Canada, and her pieces have twice been named Best in Show in their annual juried exhibitions.

Sim Luttin is a contemporary jeweler from Melbourne, Australia. She earned a BFA from the Royal Melbourne Institute of Technology and an MFA from Indiana University in metalsmithing and jewelry design. Sim exhibits in Australia, Europe, Asia, and the United States, and is represented by Charon Kransen, USA. Visit www.simluttin.com.

Susan A. Machamer has a metalsmithing degree from Syracuse University and a graduate gemologist diploma from the Gemnological Institute of America. She designs conceptual art jewelry, using a variety of precious metals and gemstones. Susan is co-owner of Cazenovia Jewelry, Inc. and an adjunct professor at Syracuse University and Cazenovia College.

Katherine Miess devotes her spare time to working in her home studio. She envelops herself in the world of jewelry and metalsmithing with periodicals, jewelry forums, blogs, and gallery visits. She dreams of, one day, making her livelihood from crafts.

Melissa Muir has been creating jewelry for several years, and her work has been featured in multiple books and publications. Melissa's philosophy is to create an atmosphere where art and jewelry play together. She shares her passion by teaching in her northeast Ohio studio. Melissa's work can be seen at www.melissamuir.com.

Karen Rakoski: engineer now retired, wire wrap inspired, natural patterns desired, design profile acquired, porcupine earrings transpired, now well-attired, 30 minutes expired. Information required? knrak@rochester.rr.com

Anjanette Randolph creates modern metal jewelry to complement the unique styles and spirits of her clients. Inspired by nature, her designs combine simple organic shapes and bright, bold colors. Her work, a product of intense imagination and mature craftswomanship, is available at www.brooklynsouljewelry.com.

Bryan and Andrea Ring are a husband and wife team who covet pieces from city streets and random locales— items like street signs and license plates. They combine their treasured findings with precious metals to create unique fine art jewelry. Each piece is fabricated in their Kansas City, Missouri, home and studio. See www.amuckdesign.com.

Davina Romansky is a metals artist incorporating the use of natural tension and movements found in nature. She gives artistic identity to each work by combining conceptual and aesthetic beauty with technical proficiency. Davina has a BFA in metals from Rochester Institute of Technology and holds numerous design awards. Website: www.davinaromansky.com.

Albrecht Scharf was born in Germany in 1972. He held an apprenticeship as a goldsmith, then spent several years as a journeyman in Nürnberg and Munich. Scharf studied at the Master School for Goldsmiths in Munich and became a master craftsman in 2004. See more of his work at www.albrecht-scharf.de.

Brenda Schweder is the author of *Junk to Jewelry* and *Vintage Redux*. A frequent *BeadStyle* contributor, Brenda has been published in all of Kalmbach's jewelry titles, as well as a number of pamphlets. Her newest book is *Steel Wire Jewelry* (Lark Books, 2011). Visit her blog at: brendaschweder.blogspot.com.

Michelle Sotolongo was born in Mexico City and raised in Houston, Texas. She received a BFA in jewelry/metals and minored in fashion merchandising at Texas State University, San Marcos, in 2007. Michelle is in constant search of creating the perfect blend between fine art and fashion. Contact her at: mm.sotolongo@gmail.com.

Jennifer Surine has a BFA in metalsmithing and jewelry making from Grand Valley State University. She resides in Michigan, where she spends most of her time with her husband, Stephen, and makes jewelry in her studio. For more information, visit www.bendthefish.com.

Amy Tavern graduated from the University of Washington in 2002 with a BFA in metal design, but now lives and works in Penland, North Carolina. She has taught beginning jewelry classes, lectured on professional practices, and currently sells her jewelry in shops and galleries around the United States. Her work is also available at www.amytavern.com.

Ingeborg Vandamme is a jewelry designer living and working in Amsterdam. She studied jewelry at the Gerrit Rietveld Academy, and now experiments with combining materials, such as paper, textiles, and metal. Her jewelry is featured in numerous Lark Books' publications: *The Art of Jewelry: Paper Jewelry, The Art of Jewelry: Wood, 500 Earrings, 500 Wedding Rings, 500 Pedants and Lockets, 500 Enameled Objects,* and *Stitched Jewels*.
Website: www.ingeborgvandamme.nl.

Federico Vianello opened his first workshop in Florence, Italy (see www.microfficina.com), and he now teaches fashion design at the university level. He hasn't exactly decided what to do when he grows up. The fact is, he uses ancient techniques, modern technology, and painstaking experimentation to create jewelry. Some of his pieces are in private or public collections, and others have been published internationally.

Victoria Walker is a jewelry designer and maker based in Cornwall, United Kingdom. Her work is inspired by a combination of movement and nature, often involving kinetic and hidden elements. Visit her online at www.vwjewellery.co.uk.

Nancy Wickman caught the jewelry bug about four years ago and has yet to find the cure. She sells her work at shows, in galleries, and online at www.wickwirejewelry.artfire.com. Nancy lives in Flushing, Michigan, with her five Boston Terriers.

Mary Jo Zeidler and Karyn Long of Milagro Metalworks in Fort Collins, Colorado, create work that combines Mary Jo's degree in archaeology with Karyn's degree in metals. Both designers agree that the textures and imagery achieved in casting inspire personal works of art. They often allude to natural landscapes as a reminder of our connection to the earth. Visit www.milagrometalworks.com or contact the designers at info@milagrometalworks.com.

ABOUT THE AUTHOR

Marthe Le Van is the senior editor for jewelry and metals at Lark Books. Since 2000, she has written, edited, juried, or curated more than 30 titles. Recent publications include *Masters: Gold—Major Works by Leading Jewelers*, and *Stitched Jewels: Jewelry That's Sewn, Stuffed, Gathered & Frayed*. She has also been the senior editor for all jewelry books in Lark's popular "500" series as well as the curator for *500 Wedding Rings*. Marthe is a member of the Society of North American Goldsmiths and the Precious Metal Clay Guild.

It's all on www.larkcrafts.com

Daily blog posts featuring needlearts, jewelry and beading, and all things crafty

Free, downloadable projects and how-to videos

Calls for artists and book submissions

A free e-newsletter announcing new and exciting books

...and a place to celebrate the creative spirit

ACKNOWLEDGMENTS

By sharing a simple workshop exercise, Robert Dancik inspired me to make this book, as I am sure he inspires countless others in their making.

The number of proposals I reviewed for this publication was record-breaking, so I want to thank all the talented designers who took the time to submit such creative ideas. Your enthusiasm and motivation are truly inspiring. To the designers whose work is included in these pages, you are at the top of your game—it amazes me that you envisioned and produced such exceptional earrings in 30 minutes or less. You're simply phenomenal.

I always appreciate the teamwork of my Lark Books colleagues. Art director Kristi Pfeffer had a fantastic vision for the layout and design of this book, and I'm so pleased with the beautiful results. Part of her vision involved a very specific photographic concept, and Stewart O'Shields delivered it flawlessly. Cover designers Chris Bryant and Celia Naranjo produced a cover that really speaks to the range of talent in this collection, and I'm grateful for their contribution. Gavin Young's editorial support was very helpful, and I appreciate her efforts. Thanks also to Chris Rich for her sharp editorial eye and to Joanna Gollberg for her technical support.

I can't sign off without thanking our readers for the excitement and passion they have for our books. I hope you find joy and inspiration in these designs. All our hard work is for your enjoyment.

DESIGNER INDEX